A LIFE C...

J.R. Miller

The building of character is the most important business of life. It matters little what works a man may leave in the world; his real success is measured by what he has wrought along the years in his own being.

True character must be built after divine patterns. Every man's life is a plan of God. There is a divine purpose concerning it which we should realize. In the Scriptures we find the patterns for all the parts of the character, not only for its great and prominent elements—but also for its most minute features—the delicate lines and shadings of its ornamentation. The commandments, the beatitudes, all Christ's precepts, the ethical teachings of the apostles—all show us the pattern after which we are to fashion our character.

It is a great thing for us to have a lofty thought of life, and ever to seek to reach it. Said Michael Angelo: "Nothing makes the soul so pure, so religious, as the endeavor to create something perfect; for God is perfection, and whoever strives for it, strives for something that is godlike." The seeking itself, makes us nobler, holier, purer, stronger. We grow ever toward that for which we long. Many searches are unrewarded. Men seek for gold—and do not find it. They try to attain happiness—but the vision ever recedes as they press toward it. The quest for true nobleness, is one that is rewarded. "Blessed are those who hunger and thirst after righteousness—for they shall be filled," is our Lord's own word. Longing for spiritual good shall never be in vain. And unceasing longing, with earnest reaching after the good, lifts the life into the permanent realization of that which is thus persistently sought.

There are certain things essential in all building. Every structure requires a good *foundation*. Without this, it never can rise into real strength and grandeur. The most beautiful building reared on sand, is insecure and must fall. There is only one foundation for Christian character. We must build on the rock; that is, we must have, as the basis of our character, great, eternal principles.

One of these principles is *TRUTH*. Ruskin tells us, that in a famous Italian cathedral there are a number of colossal figures high up among the heavy timbers, which support the roof. From the pavement, these statues have appearance of great beauty. Curious to examine them—Ruskin says he climbed one day to the roof, and stood close beside them. Bitter was his disappointment to find that only the parts of the figures which could be seen from the pavement were carefully finished. The hidden side was rough and unfinished.

It is not enough to make our lives true—only so far as *men* can see them. We have but scorn for men who profess truth, and then in their *secret life*—harbor falsehood, deception, insincerity. There must be truth through and through, in the really noble and worthy building. A little flaw, made by a bubble of air in the casting, has been the cause of the breaking of the great beam years afterward, and the falling of the immense bridge whose weight rested upon it. Truth must be in the character—absolute truth. The least falsehood mars the beauty of the life.

Another of these essential principles is *PURITY*. "Whatever things are pure," says the apostle, in the same breath with whatever things are true, and just, and honorable. It is a principle of Scripture, that a man who lives badly, can never build up a really beautiful character. Only he who has a pure heart can see God, to know what life's ideal is. Only he whose hands are clean, can build after the perfect pattern.

LOVE is another quality which must be wrought into this foundation. Love is the reverse of selfishness. It is the holding of all the life as Christ's—to be used to bless others. "So long as I have been here," said President Lincoln, after his second election, "I have not willingly planted a thorn in any man's bosom." That is one phase of love—never needlessly to give pain or do hurt to a fellow-being. The other part is the positive—to live to do the greatest good to every other being, whenever opportunity offers.

Truth, purity, love—these are the immutable principles which must be built into the foundation of the temple of character. We never can have a noble structure, without a strong and secure foundation.

On the foundation thus laid, the character must be build. No magnificent building ever grew up by *miracle*. Stone by stone it rose, each block laid in its place by toil and effort. "You cannot dream yourself into a godly character," says a writer; "you must hammer and forge yourself one." Even with the best foundation, there must be faithful, patient building unto the end.

Each one must build his own character. No one can do it for him. No one but yourself, can make your life beautiful. No one can be true, pure, honorable, and loving—for you. A mother's prayers and teachings, cannot give you strength of soul and grandeur of spirit. We are taught to edify one another, and we do, indeed, help to build up each other's life-temple. Consciously or unconsciously, we are continually leaving touches on the souls of others—touches of beauty—or of marring. In every book we read, the author lays something new on the wall of our life. Every hour's companionship with another gives either a touch of beauty—or a stain to our spirit. Every song that is sung in our ear—enters into our heart and becomes part of our being. Even the natural scenery amid which we dwell—leaves its impression upon us. Thus others, thus all things about us—do indeed have their place as builders of our character.

But we are ourselves the real builders. Others may lift the blocks into place—but we must lay them on the wall. Our own hands give the touches of beauty—or of blemish, whatever hands of others hold the brushes or mix the colors for us. If the building is marred or unsightly when it is finished—we cannot say it was some other one's fault. Others may have sinned—and the inheritance of the sin is yours. Others may have sorely wronged you—and the hurt yet stays in your life. You never can be the same in this world that you might have been, but for the wounding. You are not responsible for these marrings of your character which were wrought by others' hands. Still you are the builder—you and God.

Even the broken fragments of what seems a ruin—you can take, and with them, through God's grace, you can make a noble fabric. It is strange how many of earth's most beautiful lives, have grown up out of what seemed defeat and failure. Indeed, God seems to love to build spiritual loveliness out of the *castaway fragments of lives,* even out of *sin's debris*. In a great cathedral there is said to be a window, made by an apprentice out of the bits of stained glass that were thrown away as refuse and worthless waste, when the other windows were made—and this is the most beautiful window of all. You can build a noble character for yourself—in spite of all the hurts and injuries done to you, wittingly or unwittingly, by others—with the fragments of the broken hopes and joys, and the lost opportunities which lie strewn about your feet. No others by their worst work of hurt of marring—can prevent your building a beautiful character for yourself!

When the ancient temple of Solomon was reared, the whole world was sought through, and its most costly and beautiful things were gathered and put into the sacred house. Likewise, we should search everywhere for whatever things are true, whatever things are lovely, whatever things are pure—to build into our life. All that we can learn from books, from music, from art, from friends; all that we can gather from the Bible and receive from the hand of Christ himself—we should take and build into our character, to make it worthy. But in order to discover the things which are lovely, we must have the loveliness in our own soul. "Though we travel the world over to find the beautiful," says one, "we must carry it in our own heart, or, go where we may, we shall not find it!" Only a pure, true, loving heart—can discover the things which are true, pure, and loving to build in the character. We must have Christ in us, and then we shall find Christly things everywhere, and gather them into our own life.

There are some people who, in the discouragement of defeat and failure—feel that it is then too late for them to make their character beautiful. They have lost their last opportunity, it seems to them. But this is never true, for the people for whom Christ died. A poet tells of walking in his garden and seeing a birds' nest lying on the ground. The storm had swept through the tree and ruined the nest. While he mused sadly over the wreck of the birds' home, he looked up, and there he saw them building a new one amid the branches. The birds teach us immortals a lesson. Though all seems lost, let us not sit down and weep in despair—but let us arise and begin to build again. No one can undo a *wrong past*. No one can repair the ruins of years that are gone. We cannot live our life over again. But, at our Father's feet—we can begin anew as little children, and make all our life new.

Unfinished Life-building

"This fellow began to build—and was not able to finish!" Luke 14:30

We are all *builders*. We may not erect any house or temple on a city street for human eyes to see—but everyone of us builds an edifice which God sees! Life is a building. It rises slowly, day by day, through the years. Every new lesson we learn, lays another block on the edifice which is rising silently within us. Every experience, every touch of another life on ours, every influence that impresses us, every book we read, every conversation we have, every act of our commonest days—adds something to *the invisible building*. Sorrow, too, has its place in preparing the stones to lie on the life-wall. All of life furnishes the material.

There are many noble structures built in this world. But there are also many who build only base, shabby huts, without beauty, which will be swept away in the testing fires of judgment. There are many, too, whose life-work presents the spectacle of an *unfinished* building. There was a beautiful plan to begin with, and the work was promising for a little time—but after a while it was abandoned and left standing, with walls halfway up—a useless fragment, open and exposed, an incomplete inglorious ruin—telling no story of past splendor as do the ruins of some old castle or coliseum—a monument only of folly and failure.

One writes: There is nothing sadder than an incomplete ruin, one that has never been of use, that never was what it was meant to be, about which no pure, holy, lofty associations cling, no thoughts of battles fought and victories won, or of defeats as glorious as victories. God sees them where we do not. The highest tower, may be more *unfinished* than the lowest—to Him.

We must not forget the truth of this last sentence. There are lives which to our eyes—seem only to have been *begun* and then abandoned, which to God's eyes are still rising into more and more graceful beauty. Here is one who began his life-work with all the ardor of youth and all the enthusiasm of a consecrated spirit. For a time his hand never tired, his energy never slackened. Friends expected great things from him. Then his health gave way. The diligent hand lies folded now on his bosom. His enthusiasm no more drives him onward. His work lies *unfinished*.

"What a pity!" men say. But wait! He has not left an unfinished lifework—as God sees it. He is resting in submission at the Master's feet, and is *growing* meanwhile in the Christian graces. The spiritual temple in his soul is rising slowly in the silence. Every day is adding something to the beauty of his character as he learns the lessons of patience, confidence, peace, joy, love. His building in the end will be more beautiful, than if he had been permitted to toil on through many busy years, carrying out his own plans. *He is fulfilling God's plan for his life.*

We must not measure *spiritual* building—by *earthly* standards. Where the heart remains loyal and true to Christ; where the cross of suffering is taken up cheerfully and borne sweetly; where the *spirit* is obedient, though the *hands* must lie folded and the feet must be still—the temple rises continually toward finished beauty.

But there are *abandoned life-buildings* whose story tells only of shame and failure. Many people begin to follow Christ, and after a little time turn away from their profession, and leave only a pretentious beginning to stand as a ruin, to be laughed at by the world, and to dishonor the Master's name.

Sometimes it is **discouragement** that leads men to give up the work which they have begun. In one of his poems, Wordsworth tells a pathetic story of a *straggling heap of unhewn stones* and the beginning of a sheepfold which was never finished. With his wife and only son, old Michael, a Highland shepherd, dwelt for many years in peace. But trouble came which made it necessary that the son should go away to do for himself for a while. For a time good reports came from him, and the old shepherd would go when he had leisure and work on the sheepfold which he was building. By and by, however, sad news came from his son Luke. In the great dissolute city, he had given himself to evil ways. Shame fell on him, and he sought a hiding place beyond the seas. The sad tidings broke the old father's heart. He went about as before, caring for his sheep. To the hollow valley he would go from time to time—to build at the unfinished sheep-fold. But the neighbors in their pity noticed that he did little work in those sad days.

Years after the shepherd was gone, the remains of the unfinished sheep-fold were still there, a sad memorial of one who began to build—but did not finish. *Sorrow broke his heart—and his hand slacked.*

Too often noble life-buildings are abandoned in the time of sorrow, and the hands that were quick and skillful before grief came, hang down and do nothing more on the temple-wall. Instead, however, of leading us to give up our work and falter in our diligence—it should inspire is to yet greater earnestness in all duty, and greater fidelity in all life.

Lack of faith is another cause which leads many to abandon their life-temples, unfinished. Throngs followed Christ in the earlier days of His ministry, when all seemed bright, who when they saw the *shadow of the cross*, turned back and walked no more with Him. They lost their faith in Him. It is startling to read how near even the apostles came to leaving their buildings unfinished. Had not their faith come again after Christ arose, they would have left in this world—only sad memorials of failure, instead of glorious finished temples. In these very days there are many who through the losing of their faith, are abandoning their work on the wall of the temple of Christian discipleship, which they have begun to build. Who doesn't know those who once were earnest and enthusiastic in Christian life, while there was but little opposition—but who fainted and failed—when it became hard to confess Christ and walk with Him?

Sin in some form draws many a builder away from his work—to leave it unfinished. It may be the *world's fascinations,* which lure him from Christ's side. It may be *evil companions,* which tempt him from loyal friendship to the Savior. It may be *riches,* which enter his heart and blind his eyes to the attractions of heaven. It may be some secret debasing lust, which gains power over him and paralyzes his spiritual life. Many are those now amid the world's throngs—who once sat at the Lord's Table and were among God's people. Their lives are unfinished buildings, towers begun with great enthusiasm and then left to tell their sad story of failure to all who pass by. They began to build—and were not able to finish.

It is sad to think how much of this unfinished work, God sees as He looks down upon our earth. Think of the *good beginnings* which never came to anything in the end. Think of the *excellent resolutions* which are never carried out, the noble life-plans entered upon by so many young people with ardent enthusiasm—but soon given up. Think of the beautiful visions and high hopes which might be made splendid realities—but which fade out, with not even one earnest attempt to work them into life.

In all aspects of life we see these *abandoned buildings*. The *business* world is full of them. Men *began* to build—but in a little time they were gone, leaving their work uncompleted. They set out with enthusiasm—but became tired in time with the effort or grew disheartened at the slow coming of success, and abandoned their ideal when it was perhaps just ready to be realized.

Many *homes* present the spectacle of thousands of abandoned dreams of love. For a time, the beautiful vision shone—and two hearts tried to make it come true—but they gave it up in despair, either enduring in misery—or going their own separate ways.

So life everywhere is full of *beginnings*, which are never carried on to *completion*. There is not a soul-wreck on the streets, not a prisoner serving out a sentence behind prison bars, not a debased, fallen one anywhere—in whose soul there were not once visions of beauty, high hopes, holy thoughts and purposes and high resolves of an ideal of something lovely and noble. But alas! the visions, the hopes, the purposes, the resolves—never grew into more than *beginnings*. God bends down and sees a great wilderness of unfinished buildings, bright possibilities unfulfilled, noble *might-have-beens* abandoned; ghastly ruins now, sad memorials only of failure!

The lesson from all this—is that we should finish our work, that we should allow nothing to draw us away from our duty, that we should never become weary in following Christ, that we should persevere from the beginning of our ideals—steadfast unto the end. We should not falter under any burden, in the face of any danger, before any demand of cost or sacrifice. No discouragement, no sorrow, no worldly attraction, no hardship—should weaken for one moment our determination to be faithful unto death! No one who has begun to build for Christ—should leave an unfinished, abandoned life-work, to his own eternal grief!

Yet we must remember, unless we become discouraged, that only in a relative, human sense can any life-building be made *altogether complete*. Our best work on earth, is but marred and imperfect. It is only when we are in Christ, and are co-workers with Him, that anything we do can ever be made perfect and beautiful. But the weakest and the humblest who are simply faithful will stand at last—complete in Him. Even the merest *fragment* of life, as it appears in men's eyes, if it is truly in

Christ and filled with His love and with His Spirit—will appear finished, when presented before the divine presence. To do God's will, whatever that may be, to fill out His plan, is to be complete in Christ, even though we live but a day, and though the work we have done fills no great human plan and leaves no brilliant record among men.

The Making of Character

"A good name is more desirable than great riches; to be esteemed is better than silver or gold." Proverbs 22:1

We ought to seek to gather in this world—treasure that we can carry with us through death's gates, and into the eternal world. We should strive to build into our lives—qualities that shall endure. Men slave and work to get a little money, or to obtain honor, or power, or to win an earthly crown—but when they pass into the great vast forever, they take nothing of all this with them!

A great conqueror who had won empires and hoards of spoil, requested that he be buried with his hands uncovered, that everyone might see that his hands were empty, that he carried away with him nothing of all his vast conquests.

Yet there are things—virtues, fruits of character, graces, victories of moral conquests, which men do carry with them out of this world. Someone says: "The only thing that walks back from the tomb with the mourners and refuses to be buried—is character." This is true. What a man IS, survives him. It never can be buried. It stays about his home when his footsteps are no longer heard there. It lives in the community where he was known. And that same thing—what a man IS—he carries with him into the eternal world. Money and rank and pleasures and earthly gains—he leaves behind him; but his character, he takes with him into eternity.

This suggests at once, the importance of character and character-building. A man may not be as good as his reputation. A good reputation may hide an evil heart and life. Character is not what a man professes to be—but what he really is as God sees him. Definition is important. Reputation is not character. Reputation is what a man's neighbors and friends think of him; character is what the man is.

The history of the word 'character' is interesting. Anciently, character was the stamp or make by which a brick-maker, an engraver, or other worker *marked* the thing he made. Applied to life, character is that which one's experiences impress or print on his soul. A *baby* has no character. Its life is but a piece of white paper on which something is to be written, some song or story, perhaps a tragedy of sorrow. Character grows as the baby passes into manhood. Every day something is written here, some mark made. The *mother* writes something; the *teacher* writes something; every day's *experiences* write some words; every touch or influence of other lives—leaves some mark; temptation and struggle do their part in filling the page; books, education, sorrow, joy, companions, friends—all of life *touches* and *paints* some line of beauty—or scratches some mark of damage. Final character is the result of all these influences that work and interact upon the life. Character is the *page* fully written, the *picture* finished.

Christ's character is the model, the ideal, for every Christian life. In the end, we are to be altogether like Him; therefore all life's *aiming* and *striving* should be towards Christ's blessed beauty. His *image* we find in the Gospels. We can look at it every day. We can study it in its details, as we follow our Lord in His life among men, in all the variations of experience through which He passed.

A little Christian girl was asked the question, "What is it for you to be a Christian?" She answered, "It is to do as Jesus would do, and behave as He would behave—if He were a little girl and lived at our house." No better answer could have been given. And there is scarcely any experience of life—for which we cannot find something in Christ's life to instruct us.

We can see how Jesus did behave as a *child* in the home, as a *man* amid human needs and duties, as a *friend* with faulty and imperfect friends, as a *comforter* among sorrow-stricken ones, as a *helper* of others in their ills and infirmities. We can find the traits and qualities of His life—as they shine out in His contact with temptation, with enmity, with wrong, with pain, with sorrow.

The study of the story of Christ's life, is not like the study of a picture or marble statue; we see Christ in all human relations, and can learn just how He acted, how He bore Himself.

A child asked the mother, *"Is Jesus like anybody I know?"* It is possible to find *dim reflections* of Christ's beauty in His true followers; yet we don't need to turn to human lives, even the most perfect, to learn what Jesus was like, for we can see him in the Gospel story for ourselves. We have no excuse for not knowing what the ideal is, for a true human life.

The next thing, when we have the vision of Christ before us, is to get it implanted into our own life. Someone says, "God never yet permitted us to envision theory too beautiful for His power to make practical." This is true, and yet never without toil and struggle can we make an honorable character for ourselves. We cannot merely dream ourselves into worthy manhood or womanhood, we must forge for ourselves, with sweat and anguish, the nobleness that shall shine before God and man.

In the presence of a great painting, a young artist said to Mr. Ruskin, "Ah! if I could put such a *dream* on canvas." "Dream on canvas!" growled Ruskin. "It will take ten thousand touches of the brush on the canvas—to make your *dream* come true!"

It is easier to put on canvas the artist's dreams—than to put upon our human lives the beautiful visions of Christlikeness which we find on the Gospel pages. Yet that is the real problem of Christian living. And though hard, it is not impossible. If we but struggled and tried and worked, in our efforts to get our visions of character translated into reality, as artists do to paint their visions on canvas, or carve them in stone—we would all be very noble. Never yet has an ideal been too high to be realized at last, through the help of Christ. The heavenly visions God gives us—are prophecies of what we *may* become, what we are born *to* become.

Yet the cost is always high to carve the beauty God shows us—as an ideal for our lives. It costs self-discipline, oftentimes anguish, as we must deny ourselves, and cut off the things we love.*SELF* must be crucified if the *noble manhood* in us is ever to be set free to shine in its beauty—if the angel within the marble block is to be unimprisoned. Michelangelo used to say, as the *chips* fell thick and fast from the piece of marble in his studio, "While the marble wastes—the image grows." There must be a wasting of self, a chipping away continually of the things that are dear to our sinful human nature, if the things that are true and pure and just and lovely are to be allowed to come out in us. The marble must waste—while the image grows! It is not easy to become a godly man, a Christlike man. Yet we must never forget that it is possible. God never yet put into a soul a dream of noble character, which He is not able and ready to help make real.

The Influence of Companionship

"He who walks with the wise grows wise, but a companion of fools suffers harm." Proverbs 13:20

The power of one person's life over another's, is something almost startling! There have been single looks of an eye, which have changed a destiny. There have been meetings of only a moment, which have left impressions for life, for eternity! No one can understand that mysterious thing we call *influence*. We read of our blessed Lord, that *virtue* went out of Him and healed the timid woman who came behind Him in the crowd and touched the hem of His garment; again, when the throng surged about Him and sought to touch Him, that *virtue* went out of Him and healed them all. Of course, there never was another life such as Christ's; yet every one of us continually exerts influence—either to heal, to bless, to leave marks of beauty; or to wound, to hurt, to poison, to stain other lives.

We are forever either adding to the worlds health and happiness and good—or to its pain, sorrow, and curse. Every moment of true and honest living, every victory we win over self or sin, and even the smallest fragment of a sweet life we live—make it easier for others to he brave and true and gentle. We are always *exerting influence*.

And so it is that *companionship* always leaves its impression. One cannot even look another in the eye, in a deep, earnest gaze—but a touch has been left on his *soul*. A man, well past middle life, said that in his sensitive youth, another young man drew him aside and secretly showed him an obscene picture. He looked at it just for one moment and then turned away. But a *spot* had been burned upon his soul. The memory of that glance—he had never been able to wash out. It had come back to him along all the forty years he had lived since, even breaking in upon him in his most sacred moments, and staining his most hallowed thoughts!

We do not know what we are letting into our lives—when we take into companionship, even for one hour, one who is not good, not pure, not true. Then, who can estimate the debasing influence of such companionship, when continued until it becomes intimacy, friendship; when confidences are exchanged, when soul touches soul, when life flows into and blends with life?

When one awakens to the consciousness of the fact that he has formed or is forming a companionship with one whose influence can hurt him and perhaps destroy him—there is only one proper thing to do—it must instantly be given up!

A rabbit was caught by its foot, in the hunter's steel trap. The little creature seemed to know that unless it could get free—its life would soon be lost. So with a bravery which commands our greatest admiration, it gnawed off its leg with its own teeth, so setting itself free although leaving its foot in the trap. But who will say that it was not wiser to escape death in this manner even with the loss of its foot—than to have kept the foot and died? If anyone discovers that he is being caught in the snare of evil companionship or friendship, no matter what it may cost him—he should tear himself away from it! Better enter into pure, noble, and worthy life, with one hand or one foot, or both hands and feet cut away—than to save these members, and be dragged down to eternal death! Young people should be careful not to get caught up in *evil companionship*. It is like the machinery of a mill, which, when it once seizes even the fringe of one's clothing, quickly pulls in the whole garment, and whirls the person's body to a swift and terrible death.

But a good and honest character has also its influence. Good companionship has only blessing and benediction for another. There have been mere chance meetings, just for a moment, as when ships pass and signal each other at sea, which nevertheless have left blessings whose influence shall never perish.

So it is with the influence of good lives. Words, thoughts, songs, kindly deeds, the power of example, the inspiration of noble things—drop out of the heaven of pure friendship deep into a person's heart, and falling, are enfolded there and become beautiful gems and holy adornments in the life. Even brief moments of worthy companionship leave their mark of blessing. Then, who can tell the power of a close and long-continued friendship, running through many years, sharing the deepest experiences, heart and heart knit together, life and life woven as it were into one web?

Our *friends* are also our *ideals*. At least in every beautiful friend's life, we see some little glimpse of the heavenly life—a little fragment of the beauty of the Lord, which becomes part of the glory into which we should fashion our lives.

There is a wonderful restraining and constraining power over us—in the life of one we love. We dare not do wrong in the presence of a pure and gentle friend. Everyone knows how unworthy he feels when he comes, with the consciousness and recollection of some sin or some meanness, into the company of one he honors as a friend. It is a kind of "Jesus presence" that our friend is to us, in which we dare not do wrong.

"A friend has many functions. He comes as the brightener into our lives, to *double* our joys—and *halve* our griefs. He comes as the *counselor* to give wisdom to our plans. He comes as the *strengthener*, to multiply our opportunities and be hands and feet for us in our absence. But above all, he comes as our rebuker, to explain our failures and shame us from our sins; as our purifier, our uplifter, our ideal, whose life to us is a constant challenge in our heart! He says to us, Friend, come up higher, higher along with me; that you and I may be those truest friends, who are nearest to God when nearest to each other."

If these things are true—and no one can doubt their truth—this matter of *companionship* is one of vital importance. It is especially important for young people to give watchful thought and careful attention to the choosing of their associates and friends. Of course, they cannot choose those with whom they shall mingle in a general way, at school, or in work or business. One is often compelled to sit or stand day after day beside those who are not godly or worthy. The law of Christian love, requires that in all such cases the utmost courtesy and kindness be shown. But this can be done—and the heart not opened to real companionship.

It is companionship that leaves its mark on the life—that is, the entering into friendships in which the hearts blend. Jesus Himself showed love to all men—but He took as companions, only a few chosen ones. We are to be like Him, seeking to be a blessing to all—but receiving into personal relationships and confidences, only those who are worthy and whose lives will help in the upbuilding of our own lives.

Getting Help From Criticism

Perfection in life and character, should be the aim of every Christian. Our prayer should ever be, to be fashioned into spotless beauty. No matter what the cost may be, we should never shrink from anything which will teach us a new lesson, or put a new touch of loveliness into our character.

We get our lessons from many teachers. We read in books, fair lines which set holy tasks of attainment for us. We see in other lives, lovely things which inspire in us noble longings. We learn by experience, and we grow by exercise. We may get many a lesson, too, from those among whom we live. People ought to be a means of grace to us. Mere contact of *life with life*—is refining and stimulating. "Iron sharpens iron—so a man sharpens the countenance of his friend."

The world is not always friendly to us. It is not disposed always to pat us on the back, or to pet and praise us. One of the first things a young man learns, when he pushes out from his own home, where everybody dotes on him—is that he must submit to criticism and opposition. Not all he does receives commendation. But this very condition is healthful. Our growth is much more wholesome in such an atmosphere, than where we have only adulation and praise.

We ought to get *profit* from criticism. Two pairs of eyes should see more than one. None of us have all the wisdom there is in the world. However wise any of us may be, there are others who know some things better than we know them, and who can make valuable and helpful suggestions to us—at least concerning some points of our work. The shoemaker never could have painted the picture—but he could criticize the buckle when he stood before the canvas which the great artist had covered with his noble creations; and the artist was wise enough to welcome the criticism and quickly amend his picture, to make it correct. Of course the shoemaker knows more about shoes, and the tailor or the dressmaker more about clothes, and the furniture-maker more about furniture, than the artist does. The criticisms of these artisans on the things in their own special lines, ought to be of great value to the artist, and he would be a very foolish painter who would sneer at their suggestions and refuse to profit by them.

The same is true in other things besides are. No one's knowledge is really universal. None of us know more than a few fragments of the great mass of knowledge. There are some things somebody else knows better than you do, however wide your range of learning may be. There are very humble people who could give you suggestions well worth taking on certain matters concerning which they have more correct knowledge than you have. If you wish to make your work perfect you most condescend to take hints and information from anyone and everyone who may be ready to give it to you.

It is true, also, that others can see faults and imperfections in us—which we ourselves cannot see. We are too closely identified with our own life and work to be unprejudiced observers or just critics. We can never make the most and the best of our life, if we refuse to be taught by other than ourselves. A really *self-made man* is very poorly made, because he is the product of only one man's thought. The strong things in his own individuality are likely to be emphasized to such a degree that they become idiosyncrasies, while on other sides his character is left defective. The best-made man is the one who in his formative years has the benefit of *wholesome criticism.* His life is developed on all sides. Faults are corrected. His nature is restrained at the points where the tendency is to overgrowth, while points of weakness are strengthened. We all need, not only as a part of our education, but in all our life and work—the corrective influence of the opinions and suggestions of others.

But in order to get profit from criticism, we must relate ourselves to it in a *sympathetic* and *receptive* way. We must be ready to hear and give hospitable thought to the things that others may say of us and of what we are doing. Some people are only hurt, never helped, by criticism, even when it is most sincere. They regard it always as unkindly—and meet it with a bitter feeling. They resent it, from whatever source it may come, and in whatever form—as something impertinent. They regard it as unfriendly, as a personal assault against which they must defend themselves. They seem to think of their own life as something fenced about by such sanctities, that no other person can with propriety offer even a suggestion concerning anything that is theirs, unless it is in the way of commendation. They have such opinions of the infallibility of their own judgment, and the flawless excellence of their own performance, that it seems never to occur to them as a possibility, that the judgment of others might add further wisdom, or point out anything better. So they utterly refuse to accept criticism, however kindly, or any suggestion which looks to anything different from what they have done.

We all know people of this kind. So long as others will compliment them on their work, they give respectful attention and are pleased; but the moment a criticism is made, however slight, or even the question whether something else would not be an improvement is asked, they are offended. They regard as an enemy anyone who even intimates disapproval; or who hints, however delicately, that this or that might be otherwise.

It is hard to maintain cordial relations of friendship with such people, for no one cares to be forbidden to express an opinion which is not an echo of another's. Not many people will take the trouble to keep a lock on the door of their lips all the while, for fear of offending a self-conceited friend. Subsequently, one who rejects and resents all criticism, cuts himself off from one of the best means of growth and improvement. He is no longer teachable, and, therefore, is no longer a learner. He would rather keep his faults, than be humbled by being told of them in order to have them corrected. So he pays no heed to what any person has to say about his work, and gets no benefit whatever from the opinions and judgments of others.

Such a spirit is very unwise. Infinitely better is it, that we keep ourselves always ready to receive instruction from every source. We are not making the most of our life—if we are not eager to do our best in whatever we do, and to make constant progress in our doings. In order to do this, we must continually be made aware of the imperfections of our performances, that we may correct them. No doubt it hurts our pride to be told of our faults—but we would better let the pain work amendment, than work resentment. Really, we ought to be thankful to anyone who shows us a blemish in our life, which we then can have removed. No friend is truer and kinder to us—than be who does this, for he helps us to grow into nobler and more beautiful character.

Of course there are different ways of pointing out a fault. One person does it bluntly and harshly, almost rudely. Another will find a way to make us aware of our faults without causing us any felling of humiliation. Doubtless it is more pleasant to have our correction come in this *gentle* way. It is also the more Christian way to give it. Great wisdom is required in those who would point out faults in others. They need deep love in their own heart, that they may truly seek the good of those in whom they detect the flaws or errors, and not criticize in a spirit of exultation. Too many take*delight* in discovering faults in other people and in pointing them out. Others do it only when they are in anger, blurting out their sharp criticisms in fits of bad temper. We should all seek to possess the spirit of Christ, who was most patient and gentle in telling his friends wherein they failed.

Harm is done ofttimes, by the lack of this spirit in those whose duty it is to teach others. Paul enjoins fathers not to provoke their children to anger, lest they be discouraged. There are parents who are continually telling their children of their faults, as if their whole existence were a dreary and impertinent mistake, and as if parents can fulfill their duty to their children only by continually nagging at them and scolding them.

Those who are anointed to train and teach the young, have a tremendous responsibility for the wise and loving exercise of the power that is theirs. We should never criticize or correct—but in love. If we find ourselves in anger or cherishing any bitter, unkind, or resentful feeling, as we are about to point out an error or a mistake in another person, or in the other's work—we would better be silent and not speak—until we can speak in love. Only when our heart is full of love, are we fit to judge another, or to tell him of his faults.

But while this is the Christian way for all who would make criticisms of others, it is true also, that however we learn of our faults, however ungentle and unsympathetic the person may be who makes us aware of them—we would better accept the correction in a humble, loving way and profit by it. Perhaps few of us hear the honest truth about ourselves until someone grows angry with us, and blurts it out in bitter words. It may be an enemy who says the severe thing about us—or it may be someone who is base and unworthy of respect; but whoever it may be, we would better ask whether there may not be some truth in the criticism, and if there is—then set ourselves to correct our deficiency. In whatever way we are made aware of a fault, we ought to be grateful for the fact; for the discovery gives us an opportunity to rise to a better, nobler life, or to a higher and finer achievement.

There are people whose criticisms are not such as can profit us. It is easy to find fault, even with the noblest work. Then there are those who are instinctive fault-finders, regarding it as their privilege, almost their duty—to give an opinion on every subject which comes before them—and to offer some criticism on every piece of work that they see. Their opinions, however, are usually valueless, and ofttimes it requires much patience to receive them graciously, without showing irritation. But even in such cases, when compelled to listen to unjust and harsh criticisms from those who know nothing whatever of the matters concerning which they speak so authoritatively, we would do well to receive all criticisms and suggestions in good temper and without impatience.

An interesting story of Michael Angelo is related, which illustrates the wise way of treating even ignorant, meddlesome, and impertinent criticism. When the artist's great statue of David was placed for the first time in the Plaza in Florence, all the people were hushed in wonder before its noble majesty—all except Soderinni. This man looked at the statue from different points of view with a wise, critical air, and then suggested that the nose was a little too long. The great sculptor listened quietly to the suggestion, and taking his chisel and mallet, he set a ladder against the stature, in order to reach the face, and climbed up, carrying a little marble dust in his hand. Then he seemed to be working carefully upon the objectionable feature, as if changing it to suit his critic's taste, letting the marble dust fall as he wrought. When he came down Soderinni again looked at the figure, now from this point of view and then from that, at last expressing entire approval. His suggestion had been accepted, as he supposed, and he was satisfied.

The story furnishes a good illustration of a great deal of fault-finding to which we must listen. It is unintelligent and valueless. But it cannot be restrained. There is not subject under heaven on which these *wise people* do not claim to have a right to express an opinion, and there is no work so perfect that they cannot point out where it is faulty and might be improved. They are awed by no greatness. Such criticisms are worthy only of contempt, and such critics do not deserve courteous attention. But it is better that we treat them with patience. It helps at least in our own self-discipline, and it is the nobler way.

This, then, is the lesson—that we should not resent criticism whether it be made in a kindly or in an unkindly way; that we should be eager and willing to learn form anyone, since even the humblest and most ignorant man knows something better than we do, and is able to be our teacher at some point; that the truth always should be welcomed—especially the truth about ourselves, that which affects our own life and work—however it may wound our pride and humble us, or however its manner of coming to us may hurt us; and that the moment we learn of anything that is not beautiful in us—we should seek its correction. Thus alone, can we ever reach the best things in character, or in achievement.

Our Undiscovered Faults

"How can I know all the sins lurking in my heart? Cleanse me from my hidden faults." Psalms 19:12

The Bible speaks of sins of ignorance. So there are sins which we commit, of which we are not conscious. In one of the Psalms, there is a prayer to be cleansed from *secret* or *hidden* faults. So we have faults which are not seen by ourselves.

Then we all have in us many things, both good and bad, which our fellow-men cannot see—but of which we ourselves are aware. We cannot reveal ourselves perfectly, even to our own bosom companions. With no intention to hide anything, even desiring to live a perfectly open life, there will yet be many things in the inner depths of our being, which our nearest friends cannot discover. No one but ourselves, know the motives which actuate us. Sometimes neighbors praise our good deed—when we know well that the good was blurred by a self-seeking intent. Or others may criticize something we do, charging us with a wrong spirit—when we know in our heart, that it was true love which prompted it.

We are both *better* and *worse* than others think us to be! The *BEST* things in godly lives, do not flash their beauty before human eyes. None of us can ever show to others, all in us that is worthy. There are countless stars in the depths of the sky which no human eye ever sees. Human lives are deeper than the heavens in which the stars are set; and in the depths even of the most commonplace soul, there are more splendors unrevealed to human gaze, than are revealed. Who is there who says all the truth he tries to say, when he attempts to speak of or for his Master? What singer ever gets into his song all the music that is in his soul, when he sings? What painter ever transfers to his canvas all the loveliness of the vision which fills his heart? What Christian ever lives out all the loyalty to Christ, all the purity and holiness, all the gentleness and sweetness, all the unselfishness and helpfulness, all the grace and beauty—which he longs to show in his life? Even in those who fail and fall in defeat, and whose lives are little but shame and sin—there are yet gleams of beauty, like the shattered fragments of a once very noble ideal. We do not know what strivings, what penitences, what efforts to do better, what tears of sorrow, what hungerings after God and heaven, there are in the heart even of the depraved, in whom the world, even nearest friends, see nothing beautiful. No doubt in every life, there is some good, which human eyes cannot see.

But there is *EVIL*, also, which our friends cannot detect—things no one suspects— but of which we ourselves are painfully aware. Many a man goes out in the morning to be loved and welcomed by his friends, and praised and honored by the world— yet carrying in his own breast the memory of some deed of sin or shame committed in secret the night before! "If people only knew me," he says, "as I know myself— they would scorn me instead of trusting me and honoring me." All of us are conscious of miserable things hidden within us—secret evil habits wrought into life, the play of unholy thoughts and feelings, the rising up of ugly passions and tempers, the movements of pride, vanity, self-conceit, envy, jealousy, doubt, which do not reveal themselves to any other eye. There are evils in everyone, of which the person himself knows—but which others do not even suspect.

But there also are *FAULTS*, unlovely things and sins in our hearts, of which we ourselves are unaware. There is an eye which pierces deeper than our own into our souls. In one place Paul says, "I know nothing against myself: yet am I not hereby justified; but he who judges me is the Lord." It is not enough to be innocent of *conscious* transgression; there are sins of *ignorance*. Only God sees us through and through. We must live for *his* inspection and approval.

We cannot see our own *FAULTS*—even as our neighbors see them. The Pharisee in his prayer, which really was not a prayer at all, spoke much of other people's sins— but saw none in himself. We are all much like him. We are prejudiced in our own favor. We are very charitable and tolerant toward our own shortcomings. We make all manner of allowance for our own faults, and are wonderfully patient with our own infirmities. We see our *good* things magnified; and our *blemishes* in a light which makes them seem almost virtues. So true is this, that if we were to meet ourselves some day on the street—the self which God sees, even the self which our neighbor sees—we probably would not recognize it, as really ourselves. Our own judgment of our life, is not unmistakable. There is a self which we do not see.

Then we cannot see into the *FUTURE*, to know where the secret tendencies of our life are leading us. We do many things which to our eyes appear innocent and harmless—but which have in them a hidden evil we cannot see. We indulge ourselves in many things which to us do not appear sinful—but which leave on our soul a touch of blight, a soiling of purity—of which we do not dream. We permit ourselves many little habits in which we see no danger—but which are silently entwining their invisible threads into a strong cable, which some day shall bind us hand and foot. We omit self-denials and sacrifices, thinking there is no reason why we should make them, unaware that we are lowering our standard of living, and permitting the subtle beginnings of *self-indulgence* to creep into our heart.

There is another class of hidden faults. Sin is deceitful. No doubt there are many things in most of us—ways of living, traits of character, qualities of disposition— which we consider, perhaps, among our strong points, or at least fair and commendable things in us—which in God's eye are not only flaws and blemishes— but sins! Good and evil in certain qualities—do not lie very far apart. It is quite easy for devotion to principle—to shade off into obstinacy. It is easy for self-respect, consciousness of ability—to pass over into miserable anger, when the truth is, he is only giving way to very bad temper. It is easy to let gentleness become weakness, and tolerance toward sinners tolerance toward sin. It is easy for us to become very selfish in many phases of our conduct—while in general we are really quite unselfish.

For example: A man may be giving his life to the good of his fellows in the larger sense, while in his own home he is utterly regardless of the comfort and convenience of those nearest to him. Outside the home—he is polite, thoughtful, kindly; within the home—he cares not how much trouble he causes, exacting and demanding attention and service, and playing the *petty tyrant,* instead of the large-hearted, generous Christian. Who of us does not have *secret blemishes*—lying alongside his most *shining virtues*? We do not see them in ourselves. We see the faults cropping out in our neighbor, and we say, "What a pity, that so fine a character is so marred!" And our neighbor looks at us and says, "What a pity that with so much that is good—he has so many marring faults!" Sin is deceitful.

The substance of all that has been said is, that besides the faults our neighbors see in us, besides those our closest friends see, besides those of which we ourselves are aware—all of us have undiscovered errors in our life—hidden, secret faults, of which only God knows.

If we are living truly, we want to find every flaw or blemish there is in us—of whatever kind. He is a coward who shrinks from the discovery of his own faults. We should be glad always to learn of any hidden unloveliness in ourselves. Someone says, "Count yourself richer that day in which you discover a new fault in yourself—not richer because it is there—but richer because it is no longer a *hidden* fault; and if you have not yet found all your faults, pray to have them revealed to you, even if the revelation must come in a way which hurts your pride."

It is dangerous to allow any faults, however small—to stay in our life; but *hidden* faults are even more perilous, than those of which we are aware. They are concealed enemies, traitors in the camp, unrecognized, passing for friends! No good, true, and brave man—will allow a discovered sin of fault to stay unchallenged in his life. But undiscovered sin lurks and nests in a man's heart, and breeds its deadly evil in his very soul. Before he is aware of its presence, it may eat out the heart of his manhood, and poison the very springs of his being.

Hidden faults, remaining undiscovered and uncured in us—will hinder our spiritual growth, and we shall not know the reason for our moral weakness, or lack of power. They will also defeat the working out of the divine plan in our life. When Canove, the great sculptor, was about to begin work upon his statue of Napoleon, it is said that his keen eye saw a tiny red line running through the upper part of the splendid block of marble, out of which he was to carve the statue. The stone had been brought at great expense from Paris for this express purpose. Common eyes saw no flaw in it—but the sculptor saw it, and would not use the marble.

May it not be so ofttimes, with lives which face great opportunities? God's eye sees in them some undiscovered flaw or fault, some tiny line of marring color. God desires truth in the inward parts. The life which pleases him must be pure and white throughout. He who clings to discovered faults, refusing to cast them out—or he who refuses to let the candle of the Lord search out the hidden faults in him, that he may put them away—is marring his own destiny. God will not use him for the larger, nobler task or trust—for which he had planned to use him. The tiny red line running through the marble, causes it to be set aside and rejected. What shall we do? God alone can know our hidden faults. We must ask him to search our hearts and try our ways—and to cleanse our lives of whatever evil thing he finds in us. Our prayer should be—"Who can discern his errors? Cleanse me from hidden faults." "Search me, O God, and know my heart; test me and know my thoughts. Point out anything in me that offends you, and lead me along the path of everlasting life." Psalm 139:23-24

What is Consecration?

"Therefore, I urge you, brothers, in view of God's mercy, to offer your bodies as *living sacrifices*, holy and pleasing to God—this is your spiritual act of worship." Romans 12:1

The first condition of consecration, must always be entire readiness to *accept God's will* for our lives. It is not enough to be willing to do Christian work. There are many people who are quite ready to do *certain* things in the service of Christ—but who are not ready to do *everything* He might want them to do. Many of us have our little pet projects in Christian work, our pleasant pastimes of service for our Master, and things we like to do. Into these we enter with enthusiasm, and we suppose we are thoroughly consecrated to Christ's work, because we are so willing to do *these* things.

But the heart of consecration, is not devotion to *this* or *that* kind of service for Christ; it is devotion to the *divine will*. It is readiness to do, not what *we* want to do in Christ's service—but what *He* gives us to do. When we reach this state of spirit, we shall not need to wait long to find our work.

The next condition of consecration, resulting from this, is the *holding of our lives directly and always at the disposal of Christ*. Not only must we be willing to do His will, whatever it is—but we must actually do it. This is the *practical* part. The moment Christ wants us for any service—we must drop everything and respond to His call. *Our little plans* must be made always under His eye, as fitting into, and as parts of His perfect plan for our lives. We must make our arrangements and engagements, with the consciousness that the Master may have *other* use or work for us, and at His bidding we must give up *our* plans—for His.

We are apt to chafe at *interruptions* which break in upon our favorite work. We anticipate an unbroken day in some occupation which we have very much at heart, or perhaps a day in relaxation which we have sought in order to obtain needed rest. We hope that nothing will spoil *our dream* for that day. But the first hour is scarcely passed, before the quiet is broken. Someone calls and the call is not one that gives personal pleasure. Perhaps it is to ask some service which we do not see how we can render. Or it may seem even more needless and purposeless—a neighbor just drops in to *visit* awhile; someone without occupation comes to *pass away an hour of time* that hangs heavily. Or you are seeking rest, and there breaks in upon you a call for thought, sympathy, and help—which can be given only at much cost to yourself.

In all such cases, the *old nature rises up to protest.* We do not want to be interrupted! We want to have this whole day for the piece of *work* we are doing, or for the delightful *book* we are reading, or for the little *pet plan* we had made for it. Or we are really very *tired* and need the rest for which we have planned—and it does not seem our duty to let anything interrupt our quiet.

But you gave yourself to Christ this morning—and gave Him your day. You asked Him to prosper *your* plans—if they were *His* plans; if not, to let you know what He had for you to do. It seems clear that the calls which have so disturbed you—have some connection with your consecration and with your morning prayer. The people who called, Christ sent to you. Perhaps they need you. There may be in one,

a *discouragement* which you should change to cheer, possibly a *despair* which you should change to hope. With another it may be an hour of strong temptation, a crisis hour—and the destiny of an immortal soul may be decided in a little talk with you!

Or if there is no such need in any of those who come in and spoil your hour of quiet, perhaps the person may bring a *blessing* to you in the very *discipline* which comes in the *interruption*. God wants to train us to that condition of *readiness for His will*, that nothing He sends, no call that He makes for service—shall ever disturb us or cause one moment's chafing or murmuring. Often it takes a long while, with many lessons, to bring us to this state of *preparedness for His will.*

Once our Lord Himself took His disciples apart to rest awhile, since there were so many coming and going, that they scarcely had time to eat. But no sooner had they reached their place of resting, than the eager people, hurrying around the shore of the lake, began to gather about them, with their needs, their sorrows, and their sicknesses. Christ did not murmur when *His little plan for rest* was thus broken in upon. He did not resent the coming of the throngs, nor refuse to receive them. He did not say to them that He had come to this place for needed rest—and they must excuse Him. He forgot His weariness, and gave Himself at once, without the slightest reluctance or withholding, with all His heart's loving warmth and earnestness, to the serving and helping of the people who had followed Him, even in the most inconsiderate fashion—to His place of retirement.

From the example of our Master—we get our lesson. He may follow us to our vacation resorts, with fragments of His will. He may call us out into the darkness and the storm, on *errands of mercy* after we have worked all day, and have put on our slippers and prepared ourselves for a cozy evening of relaxation with our loved ones. He may wake us up out of our sleep by the loud ringing of the bell or phone, and call us out at midnight on some *ministry of kindness*. It seems we would have an excuse for not listening to these calls. It would not appear too unreasonable, if we should say that we are exhausted, and cannot go on these errands. There are limits to human strength and endurance. Perhaps, too, these people who want us—have no just claim on us. Besides, why didn't they send for us at an earlier hour, instead of waiting until this unreasonable hour? Or why won't *tomorrow* do? Then we shall be fresh and strong, and the *storm* will be over.

But, ordinarily, none of these answers will quite satisfy the spirit of our consecration. It is the will of God that rings our bell and calls us out. Somewhere there is a soul that needs us, and we dare not shut our ears. When the least of His little ones comes to us for any ministry—hungry to be fed, thirsty to receive a cup of cold water, in trouble to be helped—to refuse to answer the call—is to neglect Christ Himself.

Thus *true consecration* becomes very *practical*. There is no place in it, for *beautiful theories* which will not work, for *splendid visions* which will not become hands and feet in service. "Dedication meetings," with their roll-call and their Scripture verses, their pledges and their hymns, are very pleasing to God, if—if we go out to *prove* our sincerity in the *doing* of His will.

Another condition of consecration, is **humility**. It does not usually mean great things, conspicuous services—but little lowly things, for which we shall get neither praise nor thanks. Most of us must be content to live *commonplace* lives. Ninety-nine percent of the work which blesses the world, and which most advances the kingdom of Christ—must always be inconspicuous, along the lines of *common duties*, in *home relationships*, in *personal associations*, in *neighborhood helpfulness*. *Consecration* must first be a spirit in us, a spirit of love, a life in our heart, which shall flow out to everyone, in a desire to bless and help and make better.

Thackeray tells of one who kept his pocket full of acorns, and whenever he saw a vacant place in his estate, he took out one and planted it. In like manner he exhorts his readers to *speak with kind words* as they go through life, never losing a chance of saying one. "An acorn costs nothing—but it may sprout into a prodigious bit of timber." True consecration prompts and inspires us to such a life of service, and it takes humility of mind in many of us—to accept such service.

We shall never lack *guidance* in finding the duties of our consecration; if only we will follow. One day's work leads to another. One duty—opens the way to another. We are never shown *divine maps* with *all* the course of our lives projected on them—but we shall be shown always the *next* duty, and then the *next*. If only we are obedient, there shall never come a time when we cannot know what our next duty is. Those who follow Christ—shall never walk in darkness.

Making Life a Song

"Let the saints rejoice in this honor and sing for joy on their beds." Psalm 149:5

It is a great thing to *write a song* that endures. To have composed such a hymn as "Rock of Ages, Cleft for Me," or "Jesus, Lover of My Soul," is a greater achievement than to have built a pyramid. But we cannot all write songs. We are not all poets, able to weave sweet thoughts into rhythmic verse that will charm men's souls. We cannot all make hymns which shall come as messengers of peace, comfort, joy, or inspiration to weary lives. Only to a few men and women in a generation is the poet's tongue given.

But there is a way in which we may all make songs; we can make our own life a song if we will. It does not need the poet's gift and art to do this, nor does it require that we shall be taught and trained in colleges and universities. The most uneducated man may so live—that gentle music shall breathe forth from his life through all his days. He needs only to be kind and loving.*Every beautiful life is a song.*

There are many people who live in circumstances and conditions of hardness and hardship, and who seem to make no music in the world. Their lives are of that utterly prosaic kind, which is devoid of all sentiment, which has no place for sentiment amid its severe toils and under its heavy burdens. Even *home tendernesses* seem to find no opportunity for growth in the long leisureless days. Yet even such lives as these, doomed to hardest, dreariest toil—may and often do become songs which minister blessing to many others.

The other day a laborer presented himself for admission to the church. He was asked what sermon or what appeal led him to take this step. No sermon, no one's word, he answered—but a fellow-workman for years at the bench beside him had been so true, so faithful, so Christlike in his character and conduct, that his influence had brought his companion to Christ. This man's life, amid all its hardness, was a sweet song of love.

A visitor to an old European city desired to hear the wonderful chimes which were part of the city's fame. Finding the church, he climbed up into the tower-supposing that to be the way to hear the sweet music of the chimes. There he found a man who wore heavy wooden gloves on his hands. Soon this man went to a rude keyboard and began to pound on the keys. There was a terrible clatter as the wood struck the keys, and close over head there was a deafening crash and clangor among the bells as they were pounded upon by the heavy hammers. But there was no sweet music. The tourist soon fled away from the place, wondering why men came so far to listen to this noisy hammering and this harsh clanging. Meanwhile, however, there floated out over the city from the bells in the tower the most exquisite music. Men working in the fields far off heard it and paused to listen to it. People in their homes, and at their work, and on the streets were charmed by the marvelous sweetness of the rich bell-tones that dropped upon their ears.

There are many people whose lives have their best illustration in the work of the old chine-ringer. They are shut up in narrow spheres. They must give all their strength to hard toil. They dwell continually amid the noise and clatter of the most common work. They seem to their friends to be doing nothing with their lives, but striking heavy hammers on noisy keys. They make no music—only a deafening clatter at the best. They do not dream themselves that they are making any music for the world. Yet all the while, as they live true, patient, honest, unselfish and helpful lives—they are putting *cheer* and *strength* and *joy* in other hearts. A little home is blessed by their love, its needs provided for by their hard work. Future generations may be better and happier, because of some influence or ministry of theirs. From such families many of the world's greatest and best men have sprung. Thus, as with the chimes, the clatter and clangor that the life makes for those who stand close beside—become gentle songs and quiet music to those who listen farther away.

God wants all our lives to be songs. He gives us the *words* in the duties and the experiences of our lives which come to us day by day, and it is our part to set them to *music* through our obedience and submission. It makes a great deal of difference in music, how the notes are arranged on the staff. To scatter them along the lines and spaces without order, would make only bars of sad discord. They must be put upon the staff according to the rules and principles of harmony, and then they make beautiful music.

It is easy to set the notes of life on the staff so that they shall yield only enervating discord. Many people do this, and the result is discontent, unhappiness, distrust and worry, for themselves; and in their relations to others, bitterness, strife, wrangling. It is our duty, whatever the notes may be that God gives to us, whatever the words He writes for us to sing, to make harmonious music. Jesus said, "My *peace* I give unto you" (John 14:27). An inspired promise reads: "The *peace* of God shall keep your heart and mind through Christ Jesus" (Phil. 4:7). A heavenly counsel is: "Let the peace of God rule in your heart" (Col. 3:15). Whatever the notes or the words, therefore, the song which we sing should be *peace*.

A perfectly holy life would be a perfect song. At the best while on earth, our lives are imperfect in their harmonies—but if we are Christ's disciples, we are *learning to sing* while here, and someday the music will be perfect. It grows in beauty and sweetness here just as we learn to do God's will on earth as it is done in heaven.

Only the *Master's hand*, can bring out of our souls the music that slumbers in them. A violin lies on the table silent and without beauty. One picks it up and draws the bow across the strings—but it yields only wailing discords. Then a *master* comes and takes it up, and he brings from the little instrument, the most marvelous music. Other men touch our lives and draw from them only jangled notes; Christ takes them, and when He has put the chords in tune—He brings from them the music of love and joy and peace.

It is said that once Mendelssohn came to see the great Freiburg organ. The old custodian refused him permission to play upon the instrument, not knowing who he was. After much persuasion, however, he granted him permission to play a few notes. Mendelssohn took his seat, and soon the most wonderful music was breaking forth from the organ. The custodian was spellbound. At length he came up beside the great musician and asked his name. Learning it, he stood humiliated, self-condemned, saying, "And I refused you permission to play upon my organ." There comes One to us who desires to take our lives and play upon them. But we withhold ourselves from Him, and refuse Him permission, when if we would only yield ourselves to Him, He would bring from our souls heavenly music.

Come what may, we should make our lives songs. We have no right to add to the world's discords, or to sing anything but sweet strains in the ears of others. We should play no note of sadness in this world, which is already so full of sadness. We should add something every day to the stock of the world's happiness. If we are really Christ's, and walk with Him, we cannot but sing.

Making Life Music in Chorus

"Make my joy complete by being like-minded, having the same love, being one in spirit and purpose." Philippians 2:2

There is more to be said about *making life a song*. Each one of us should so live—as to make music in this world. This we can do by simple, cheerful obedience. He who does God's will faithfully each day, makes his life a song. The music is peace. It has no jarring dissonance, no anxieties or worries, no rebellions or doubts.

But we must make music also *in relation to others*. We do not live alone; we live with others, in families, in friendship's circles, in communities. It is one thing for a singer to sing solos, and to sing sweetly, sincerely in perfect time, in harmonious proportion; and quite another thing for several people to sing together, in choir or chorus, and their voices all to blend in harmony. It is necessary in this latter case that they should all have the *same key* and that they should sing carefully, each listening to the others and controlling or repressing or restraining his own voice for the sake of the effect of the whole full music. If one sings independently, out of tune, or out of time—he mars the harmony of the chorus. If one sings without regard to the other voices, only for the display of his own—his part is out of proportion and the effect is discord.

It is necessary not only that we make sweet music in our individual lives—but also that in choirs or choruses we produce pleasing harmony. Some people are very good *alone*, where no other life comes in contact with theirs, where they are entirely their own master and have to think only of themselves—but make a wretched business of living—when they come into relationships with others. There they are selfish, tyrannical, despotic, willful. They will not tolerate suggestion, request, or authority. They will not make any compromise, will not yield their own opinions, preferences, or prejudices, and will not submit to any inconvenience, any sacrifice.

But we are not good Christians, until we have learned to live harmoniously with others, for example, in the family. A true marriage means the ultimate bringing of two lives into such perfect oneness that there shall not be any discord in the blended music. To attain this, each must give up much. There must be on the part of both, self-repression and self-renunciation. The aim of each must be, what always is true love's aim—to serve the other. Only in perfect love, which is utterly self-forgetful, can there be perfect blending.

Then, as a family grows up in the home, it is harder still to keep the music without dissonance, with the varying individual tastes and preferences which are disposed to assert themselves often in aggressive ways. It can be done only by keeping love always the ruling motive. But there are families that never do learn to live together lovingly. Oftentimes the harmony is spoiled by *one member* of the household who will not yield to the sway of unselfishness, or repress and deny *SELF* for the good of all. On the other hand, in homes that do grow into the closeness of love, there is frequently one life that by its calm, patient, serene peace that nothing can disturb, at length draws all the discordant elements of the household life into accord with itself, and so perfects the music of the home.

In all relations, the same lesson must somehow be learned. We must learn to live with people—and live with them *sweetly!* And people are not all kind and gentle. Not many of them are willing to do all the yielding, all the giving up or sacrificing. We must each do our share—if we are to live congenially with others. Some people's idea of giving up—is that the other person must do it all. That is what some *despotic husbands* think their wives ought to do. In all associated life, there is this same tendency to let the *yielding* be by the *other* person. "We get along splendidly," a man says, referring to his business, or to some associated work. "So-and-so is very easy to live with. He is gentle and yielding, and always gives up. So I have things my own way, and we get along together beautifully." Certainly—but that is not the Christian way. The self-repression and self-renunciation should be *mutual*. "Love each other with genuine affection, and take delight in honoring each other," is Paul's rule. When each person in any association of living does this, seeking the honor and promotion of the other, not thinking of himself—the music is full of harmony. The essential thing in *love* is not receiving—but *giving*; not the desire to be helped or honored—but to help or honor.

Then not in our *relationships* only—but in *circumstances* also, must we learn to make our lives a song. This is not hard when all things are to our liking, when we are in prosperity, when friends surround us, when the family circle is unbroken, when health is good, when there are no crosses, and when no self-denials are required. But it is not so easy—when the flow of pleasant circumstances is rudely broken, when sorrow comes, when bitter disappointment dashes away the hopes of years. Yet Christian faith can keep the music unbroken, even through such experiences as these. The music is changed. It grows more *tender*. Its tones become *deeper*, tremulous sometimes, as the tears creep into them. But it is really *enriched* and made more *mellow* and *beautiful*.

There is a story of a German baron who stretched wires from tower to tower of his castle to make a great Aeolian harp. Then he waited and listened for the music. For a time the air was still, no sound was heard. The wires hung silent in the air. After a while there came gentle breezes, and then *soft strains of music* were heard. At length the cold wintry winds blew storm-like in their wild fury; then the wires gave forth majestic music.

Our lives are harps of God—but many of them do not give out their sweetest music in the *calm* of quiet, prosperous days. It is only in the *heavy storm* of trial, in adversity, in grievous pain or loss—that the richest, most majestic music comes from our souls. Most of us have to learn our best and most valuable lessons—in the stress of affliction.

We should seek to have our lives so trained, so disciplined, that no sudden *change of circumstances* shall ever stop its music; that if we are carried out of our summer of joy today—into a winter of grief tomorrow, the song shall still go on—the song of faith, love, peace. Paul had *learned* this when he could say, "I have learned to be content whatever the circumstances. I know what it is to be in need, and I know what it is to have plenty. I have learned the secret of being content in any and every situation, whether well fed or hungry, whether living in plenty or in want. I can do everything through him who gives me strength. Philippians 4:11-13. Circumstances did not affect him, for the source of his peace and joy was in Christ.

How can we get these lessons? There is an old legend of a musical *instrument* that hung on a castle wall. Its strings were broken. It was covered with dust. No one understood it, and none could put it in order. But one day a stranger came to the castle. He saw the instrument on the wall. Taking it down, he quickly brushed the webs and dust from it, tenderly reset the broken strings, then played upon it. The chords long silent, woke beneath his touch—and the castle was filled with rich music.

Every human life in its unrenewed state is such a harp, with broken strings, tarnished by sin. It is capable of giving forth music marvelously rich and majestic— but first it must be restored, and the only one who can do this—is the Maker of the harp, the Lord Jesus Christ. Only He can bring the jangled chords of our lives into tune, so that when played upon, they shall give forth sweet music. We must, therefore, surrender our hearts to Him, that He may repair and restore them. Then we shall be able to make music, not in our individual lives only—but in whatever relations or circumstances our lot may be cast!

The Beauty of the Lord

"Let the *beauty of the Lord* our God be upon us!" Psalm 90:17

When Charles Kingsley was dying, he seemed to have a glimpse of the heavenly splendor into which he was going, and of God in His brightness and loveliness, and he exclaimed, "How beautiful God is!"

Every revelation of *God* that is made to us—is a revelation of *beauty*. Everywhere in nature, in the *flower* that blooms, in the *bird* that sings, in the *dewdrop* that sparkles, in the *star* that shines, in the *sunset* that burns with splendor—we see reflections of God's beauty. "He has made *everything beautiful* in its time!" (Ecclesiastes 3:11). In the holy Scriptures, every revelation of the divine *character* presents God to us in surpassing loveliness. Christ was "God manifest in the flesh" (1 Timothy 3:16), the beauty of the invisible God made visible to human eyes, and such enrapturing beauty has never been seen, except in that one blessed life.

The beauty of God is frequently referred to in the Scriptures. In one of

his Psalms David declared that the supreme desire of his heart, was to dwell in the house of the Lord all the days of his life, to behold the beauty of the Lord.

Then, in the prayer of Moses, we have the petition, "Let the beauty of the Lord our God be upon us." This was a prayer that the charm of God's excellence, might be given to His people, that the divine beauty might shine in them, in their lives, in their faces, in their souls. We think of the face of *Moses* himself, when he came down from the mountain after his forty days communing with God. He had been so long wrapped in the divine glory—that his very body was as it were, saturated with its brightness. Or we think of *Stephen*, before his martyrdom, when a window of heaven was opened and a ray of the glory from the holy place fell on him, so irradiating his features that even to his enemies, they appeared like the features of an angel.

There is a *beauty of soul* which makes the plainest face radiant, and the homeliest features lovely; which shines like a star in this world of sin. It is for this beauty that we are taught to pray, "Let the beauty of the Lord our God be upon us." It is not the beauty which fades—when sickness smites the body; or which is lost in the withering touch of years; or which blanches when death's pallor overspreads the features. But this is a beauty which grows lovelier in pain or suffering, which shines out in sorrow like a star in the night, which transfigures the wrinkled and faded features of old age—and which bursts out in death into the full likeness of Christ!

Every Christian life is beautiful—so far as it fairly and truly represents Christ. Anything in religion that is not beautiful, is not a just or adequate expression of the divine thought. Holiness of character is simply the reproduction in human life—of the likeness of Christ, and any feature that is not lovely and winning, is not truly Christlike, and hence misrepresents Christ. It is not the Christian religion itself that is unlovely in any case—but the human interpretation of it in disposition and conduct.

There are certain qualities that belong to the beauty of the Lord whenever it appears in any life. One of these is *spiritual thirst*. The eyes look upward and beyond the things of earth. The heart is fixed on things above. The aspiration is for *more holiness*, and finds expression in such yearnings as "Nearer, my God, to Thee," and "More love, O Christ, to Thee," and in the prayer, "Let the beauty of the Lord our God be upon us."

A faith that is satisfied with any *ordinary attainments*, or that is ever satisfied at all, is not a living faith. The Master's benediction is upon those who hunger and thirst after righteousness. The *longing* soul is the *healthy* soul. Spiritual longing is the heart's cry which God always hears and answers with more and more of His fullness. Such longing is the ascending angel that climbs the *starry ladder*, to return on the same radiant stairway, with ever new blessings from God. It is nothing less than the very life of God in the human soul, struggling to grow up into the fullness of the stature of Christ. It is the transfiguring spirit in us—which cleanses these dull earthly lives of ours and changes them little by little into the divine image.

But the beauty of the Lord in a human life, is not *merely* a heavenly yearning. It is intensely *practical*. It is more than *religious sentimentality*, more than *devout feeling*, more than *holy aspiration*. True spiritual longing draws the whole life upward with it. Joan of Arc said that her white standard was so victorious because she followed it *herself*. We must have our spiritual *aspirations*—but we must *follow* them ourselves if we would make our lives beautiful. True holiness does not make people unsuitable for living well in this world. It has its *visions* of Christ—but it brings them down to brighten its *daily path* and to become *inspirations to beautiful living*. It has its joyful emotions—but they become impulses to self-denial and patient work for the Master.

One of the first results of grace in the heart—is sweeter, kindlier, truer, more helpful living, in all life's common relations. It makes a man a kinder neighbor, a more thoughtful husband, a gentler father. A Christian *girl*, whose religion does not make her a better daughter and a more loving, patient sister—does not have the right concept of Christ. A *wife* and mother shows the beauty of holiness, not only in her earnestness in prayer and church work—but in her devotion to the interests of her home. Mrs. Prentiss said: "A mother can pray with a sick child on her lap more acceptably, than if she left it alone in order to go and pray by herself."

In was said of *Francesca,* that though unwearied in her devotions, yet if, during her prayers she was called away by her husband or by any domestic duty, she would close the book cheerfully, saying that a wife and a mother, when called upon, must cease to serve God at the *altar*—to serve Him in her *domestic duties.*

Heavenly contemplation must not draw us away from *earthly duty.* When we get to heaven, we shall find heavenly work to do—but for the present our duty is here on earth, and he is the best Christian who does it best. We do not want a religion that will lift us up into a seventh heaven of rapture, making us forget our *duties* to those about us—but a religion that will bring God down to walk with us on all the hard paths of toil and struggle, and that will lead us out into a gentle and patient ministry of love.

It is the fashion to praise *Mary*—and censure *Martha.* Jesus blamed Martha's *worry*—but not her *service.* It is good to sit at the Master's feet. The piety which best pleases Christ—is that which waits most lovingly at His feet to receive blessing and strength—and then goes forth, diligent in all love's duties and fidelities.

One other feature of the beauty of the Lord, as worn by His children on the earth—is moral **purity.** Christ's benediction is for the *pure in heart. Bodily* health is beautiful, *mental* ability is beautiful—but *heart purity* is the charm of all. All spiritual loveliness begins within. That the beauty of the Lord our God may be on us, that the winning charm of God's loveliness may shine in the features of our lives which men can see—we must first have the *divine beauty within us.* A *holy heart* will in time transfigure all the life. And the only way to have a holy heart—is to have Christ within!

Getting Christ's Touch

"Again Jesus said—Peace be with you! As the Father has sent me, I am sending you." John 20:21

There was wonderful power in the *touch of Christ* when He was on the earth. Wherever He laid His hand—He left a blessing. *Virtue* went out of Him, each time He touched the sick, sad, and weary ones, always giving health, comfort, and peace. That hand, glorified, now holds in its clasp the seven stars. Yet there is a sense in which the blessed touch of Christ is felt yet on the earth. He is as truly in this world today—as He was when He walked through Judea and Galilee in human form! He is with each one of His people. His parting promise was: "I am with you *all the days.*" (Matthew 28:20).

The hand of Christ is still laid on the weary, the suffering, the sorrowing, and though its *pressure* is unfelt, its *power* to bless is the same as in the ancient days. It is laid on the *sick*—when precious heavenly words of cheer and encouragement from the Scriptures are read at their bedside, giving them sweet patience and quieting their fears. It is laid on the *sorrowing*—when the consolations of divine love come to their hearts with blessed comfort, giving them strength to submit to Gods will and rejoice in the midst of trial. It is laid on the *faint* and *weary*—when the grace of Christ comes to them with its holy peace, hushing the wild tumult and giving calm rest of soul.

There is another way in which the hand of Christ is laid on human lives. He sends His disciples into the world to *represent* Him. "As the Father has sent me, I am sending you" (John 20:21), is His own word. Of course the best and holiest Christian life can be only the dimmest, faintest reproduction of the rich, full, blessed life of Christ. Yet it is in this way, through these *earthen vessels*, that He has ordained to save the world, and to heal, help, comfort, lift up and build up men.

Perhaps in thinking of what God does for the world, we are too apt to overlook the *human instruments* and think of Him touching lives directly and immediately. A friend of ours is in sorrow, and going to our knees we pray God to send comfort. But couldn't it be—that He would send the comfort through our own hearts and lips? One we love is not doing well, is drifting away from the Christian life, is in danger of being lost. In anguish of heart we cry out to God, beseeching Him to lay His hand on the imperiled life and rescue it. But could it not be—that our's is the hand that must be stretched out in love, and laid in Christ's name on the life that is in danger?

It is certain, at least, that each one of us who knows the love of Christ, is ordained to be as Christ to others; that is, to show to them the spirit of Christ, the patience, gentleness, thoughtfulness, love, and yearning of Christ. We are taught to say "Christ lives in me." If this is true, Christ loves others through us—and our touch must be to others, as the very touch of Christ Himself. Every Christian ought to be, in a human measure, a *new incarnation of the Christ*, so that people shall say: "He interprets Christ to me. He comforts me in my sorrow as Christ Himself would do—if He were to come and sit down beside me, and is as helpful and patient as Christ would be—if He were to return and take me as His disciple."

But before we can be in the place of Christ to sorrowing, suffering, and struggling ones, we must have the mind in us, which was in Him. When Paul said, "The love of Christ constrains me" (2 Cor. 5:14), he meant that he had the very love of Christ in him—the love that *loved* even the most unlovely, that *helped* even the most unworthy, that was *gentle* and affectionate even to the most loathsome. We are never ready to do good in the world, in a real sense, or in any large measure—until we have become thus filled with the very spirit of Christ.

We may try help people in a certain way—without loving them. We may render them services of a certain kind, benefiting them externally or temporally. We may put gifts into their hands, build them houses, purchase clothing for them, carry them food, or improve their circumstances and condition. In such a manner, we may do many things for them, without having any *sincere love* in our hearts for them. Yet this is nothing better than *common philanthropy*. But the highest and most real help we can give them—is only through loving them.

There is a touching and very illustrative story of a good woman in Sweden who opened a home for crippled and diseased children—children for whom no one else was ready to care. Eventually she received into her home about twenty of these unfortunate little ones. Among them was a boy of three years, who was a most frightful and disagreeable object. He resembled a skeleton. His skin was covered with hideous blotches and sores. He was always whining and crying. This poor little fellow gave the good lady more care and trouble, than all the others together. She did her best for him. But the child was so *repulsive* in his looks and ways, that, try as she would, she could not bring herself to *like* him, and often her *disgust* would show itself in her face, in spite of her effort to hide it. She could not really *love* the child.

One day she was sitting on the verandah steps with this child in her arms. The sun was shining brightly and the perfume of the autumn honeysuckles, the chirping of the birds, and the buzzing of the insects, lulled her into a sort of sleep. Then in a half-waking, half-dreaming state, she thought of herself as having changed places with the child, and as lying there—only more foul, more repulsive than he was.

Over her she saw the Lord Jesus bending, looking lovingly into her face, yet with an expression of gentle rebuke in His eye, as if He meant to say, "If I can bear with you, who are so full of sin—surely you ought, for My sake, to love that poor suffering child."

She woke up with a sudden startle, and looked into the boy's face. He had awakened too, and he looked earnestly into her face. Sorry for her past repulsion, and feeling in her heart a new compassion for him, a new love springing up into her bosom for him—she bent her face to his and kissed him as tenderly as ever she had kissed a baby of her own. With a startled look in his eyes, and a flush on his cheeks, the boy gave her back a smile so sweet—that she had never seen one like it before. From that moment, a wonderful change came over the child. He understood the new love that had come, instead of dislike and loathing, in the woman's heart. That touch of human love transformed his peevish, fretful nature—into gentle quiet and beauty. The woman had seen a vision of herself in that blotched, repulsive child—and of Christ's wonderful love for her in spite of her sinfulness. Under the inspiration of this vision—she had become, indeed, *Christ* to the child. The love of Christ had come into her heart.

Christ loves the unlovely, the loathsome, the deformed, the leprous. We have only to think of ourselves as we are in His sight, and then remember that, in spite of all the moral and spiritual loathsomeness in us—He yet loves us, does not shrink from us, lays His hand upon us to heal us. This Christian woman had seen a vision of herself, and of Christ loving her by condescending to bless her and save her; and now she was ready to *be Christ*, to show the spirit of Christ, to be the love of Christ—to this poor loathsome child lying on her knee.

She had gotten the "*touch* of Christ" by getting the *love* of Christ in her heart. And we can get it in no other way. We must see ourselves as Christ's servants, to be to others—what He is to us. Then shall we he enabled to bless every life which our lives touch. Our *words* shall throb with love, and will find their way to the hearts of the weary and sorrowing. There will be a sympathetic thrill in our *lives*—which will give a strange power of helpfulness to whatever we do. Everywhere around us, there are lives which, by the touch of our hand, in loving warmth, in Christ's name—would be wondrously blessed.

Someone tells of going into a jeweler's store to look at certain gems. Among other stones, he was shown an *opal*. As it lay there, however, it appeared dull and altogether lusterless. Then the jeweler took it in his hand and held it for some moments, and again showed it to his customer. Now it gleamed and flashed with all the glories of the rainbow. It needed the touch and the warmth of a human hand, to bring out its iridescence. There are human lives everywhere around us, that are rich in their possibilities of beauty and glory. No gems or jewels are so precious. But as we see them they are dull and lusterless, without brightness. Perhaps they are even covered with stain, and defiled by sin. Yet they need only the *touch of the hand of Christ*—to bring out the radiance, the loveliness, the beauty, of the divine image in them. And you and I must be the hand of Christ—to these lusterless or stained lives!

The Blessing of Weakness

"But he said to me, 'My grace is sufficient for you, for my power is made perfect in *weakness*.' Therefore I will boast all the more gladly about my *weaknesses*, so that Christ's power may rest on me. That is why, for Christ's sake, I delight in *weaknesses*, in insults, in hardships, in persecutions, in difficulties. For when I am *weak*, then I am strong."
2 Corinthians 12:9-10

We are not accustomed to think of *weakness*—as a condition of blessing. We would say, "Blessed is *strength*. Blessed are the strong." But Bible beatitudes are usually the reverse of what nature would say. "Blessed are the meek." "Blessed are you when men shall reproach you." The *law of the cross* lies deep in spiritual life. It is by the crucifying of the flesh—that the spirit grows into beauty. So, "Blessed are the weak—for they shall have God's strength," is a true scriptural beatitude, although its very words are not found in the Bible.

Weakness is blessed, because it insures to us more of the sympathy and help of Christ. Weakness ever appeals to a gentle heart. We see illustrations of this truth in our common human life. What can be more weak and helpless than blindness? Here is a blind child in a home. Her condition seems pitiable. She gropes about in darkness. She is unaware of dangers that may beset her, and cannot shield herself from any harm which threatens her. The windows through which others see the world—to her are closed, and she is shut up in darkness. She is almost utterly helpless. Yet her very weakness is her strength. It draws to itself the best love and help of the whole household. The mother's heart has no such tender thought for any of the other children—as for the blind girl. The father carries her continually in his affection and is ever doing gentle things for her. Brothers and sisters strive in all ways to supply her lack. The result is that no other member of the family is sheltered so safely as she is, and that none is half so strong. Her very *helplessness* is the secret of her *strength*. Her closed eyes and outstretched hands and tottering feet appeal resistlessly to all who love her, inspiring them to greater thoughtfulness and helpfulness towards her—than anyone else in the household.

This illustrates also—God's special thought and care for the weak. All the best things in human life, are really hints and gleams of the divine life. The heart of Christ goes out in peculiar interest toward the weak. Paul could well afford to keep his "thorn" with its burdening weakness, because it made him far more the object of divine sympathy and help. So weakness always makes strong appeal to the divine compassion. We think of suffering or feebleness as a misfortune. It is not altogether so, however, if it makes us dearer and brings us nearer to the heart of Christ. Blessed is weakness, for it draws to itself the strength of God!

Weakness is blessed, also, because it saves from spiritual peril. Paul tells us that his "thorn" was given to him to keep him humble. Without it he would have been exalted over much and would have lost his spirituality. We do not know how much of his deep insight into the things of God, and his power in service for his Master, Paul owed to this torturing "thorn." It seemed to hinder him and it caused him incessant suffering—but it detained him in the low valley of humility, made him ever conscious of his own weakness and insufficiency, and thus kept him near to Christ whose home is with the humble.

Spiritual history is full of similar cases. Many of God's noblest servants have carried "thorns" in their flesh all their days—but meanwhile they have had spiritual blessing and enrichment which they never would have had, if their cries for relief had been granted. We do not know what we owe to the sufferings of those who have gone before us. *Prosperity* has not enriched the world—as *adversity* has done. The best thoughts, the richest life lessons, the sweetest songs that have come down to us from the past—have not come from lives that have known no privation, no adversity—but are the fruits of pain, of weakness, of trial. Men have cried out for emancipation from the bondage of hardship, of sickness, of infirmity, of self-denying necessity; not knowing that the thing which seemed to be hindering them in their career—was the very making of whatever was noble, beautiful, and blessed in their life.

There are few people who have not some "thorn" rankling in their flesh. In one it is an infirmity of speech, in another an infirmity of sight, in another an infirmity of hearing. Or it may be lameness, or a disease, slow but incurable, or constitutional timidity, or excessive nervousness, or a disfiguring bodily deformity, or an infirmity of temper. Or it may be in one's home, which is cold, unloving, and uncongenial; or it may be in the life of a loved one—sorrow or moral failure; or it may be a bitter personal disappointment through untrue friendship or love unrequited. Who has not his "thorn"?

We should never forget that in one sense our "thorn" is a "messenger of Satan," who desires by it to hurt our life, to mar our peace, to spoil the divine beauty in us, to break our communion with Christ. On the other hand, however, Christ himself has a loving design in our "thorn." He wants it to be a blessing to us. He would have it keep us humble—and save us from becoming vain; or he means it to soften our hearts and make us more gentle. He would have the uncongenial things in our environment discipline us into heavenly-mindedness, give us greater self-control, help us to keep our hearts loving and sweet amid harshness and unlovingness. He would have our pain teach us endurance and patience, and our sorrow and loss teach us faith.

That is, our "thorn" may either be a blessing to us, or it may do us irreparable harm—which, it depends upon ourselves. If we allow it to fret us; if we chafe, resist, and complain; if we lose faith and lose heart—it will spoil our life. But if we accept it in the faith that in its ugly burden, it has a blessing for us; if we endure it patiently, submissively, unmurmuringly; if we seek grace to keep our heart gentle and true amid all the trial, temptation, and suffering it causes—it will work good, and out of its bitterness will come sweet fruit. The responsibility is ours, and we should so relate ourselves to our "thorn" and to Christ, that growth and good, not harm and marring, shall come to us from it. Such weakness is blessed only if we get the victory over it, through faith in Christ.

"But He said to me, 'My grace is sufficient for you, for my power is made perfect in weakness.' Therefore I will boast all the more gladly about my weaknesses, so that Christ's power may rest on me. That is why, for Christ's sake, I delight in weaknesses, in insults, in hardships, in persecutions, in difficulties. For when I am weak—then I am strong." 2 Corinthians 12:9-10. There is a blessing in weakness, also, because it nourishes dependence on God. When we are strong, or deem ourselves strong, we are really weak, since then we trust in ourselves and do not seek divine help. But when we are consciously weak, knowing ourselves unequal to our duties and struggles, we are strong, because then we turn to God and get his strength.

Too many people think their weakness is a barrier to their usefulness, or make it an excuse for doing little with their life. Instead of this, however, if we give it to Christ, he will transform it into strength. He says his strength is made perfect in weakness; that is, what is lacking in human strength he fills and makes up with divine strength. Paul had learned this when he said he gloried now in his weaknesses, because on account of them the strength of Christ rested upon him, so that, when he was weak, then he was strong—strong with divine strength.

The people who have done the greatest good in the world, who have left the deepest, most abiding impression upon the lives of others, have not been those whom the world called the strong. Much of the world's best work has been done by the weak, by those with broken lives. Successful men have piled up vast fortunes, established large enterprises, or won applause in some material way; but the real influence that has made the world better, enriched lives, taught men the lessons of love, and sweetened the springs of society, has come largely, not from the strong—but from the weak.

I walked over a meadow and the air was full of delicious fragrance. Yet I could see no flowers. There was tall grass waving on all sides—but the fragrance did not come from the grass. Then I parted the grass and looked beneath it, and there, close to the earth, hidden out of sight by the showy growths in the meadow, were multitudes of lowly little flowers. I had found the secret of the sweetness—it poured out from these humble hiding flowers. This is a picture of what is true everywhere in life. Not from the great, the conspicuous, the famed in any community, comes the fragrance which most sweetens the air—but from lowly lives, hidden, obscure, unpraised, which give out the aroma of unselfishness, of kindness, of gentleness. In many a home it is from the room of an invalid, a sufferer—that the sweetness comes, which fills all the house. We know that it is from the cross of Christ, that the hallowing influence flowed which all these centuries has been*refining* and *enriching* and *softening* the world's life. So it is always—out of weakness and suffering, and from crushed, broken lives—comes the blessing which renews and heals the world.

"The healing of the world

Is in its nameless saints."

We need only to make sure of one thing—that we do indeed bring our weakness to Christ and lean on him in simple faith. This is the vital link in getting the blessing. Weakness itself is a burden; it is chains upon our limbs. If we try to carry it alone—we shall only fail. But if we lay it on the strong Son of God—and let him carry us and our burden, going on quietly and firmly in the way of duty—He will make our very weakness, a secret source of strength. He will not take the weakness from us—that is not his promise—but he will so fill it with his own power that we shall be strong, more than conquerors, able to do all things through Christ who strengthens us!

This is the blessed secret of having our burdening weakness, transformed into strength. The secret can be found only in Christ. And in Him--it can be found by every humble, trusting disciple.

We ought not to allow ourselves to be beaten in living. It is the privilege and duty of every believer in Christ to live victoriously. No man can ever reach noble Christian character, without sore cost in pain and sacrifice. All that is beautiful and worthy in life—must be won in struggle. The crowns are not put upon men's heads through the caprice or favoritism of any king; they are the reward of victorious achievement. We can make life easy, in a way, if we will—by shirking its battles, by refusing to grapple with its antagonisms; but in this way we never can make anything *beautiful* and *worthy* of our life. We may keep along shore with our craft, never pushing out into deep waters; but then we shall never discover new worlds, not learn the secret of the sea. We may spare ourselves costly service and great sacrifices, by saving our own life from hardships, risks, and pain—but we shall miss the blessing which can come only through *the losing of self.* "No cross—no crown" is the law of spiritual attainment.

"He who has never a conflict—has never a victor's palm,

And only the toilers—know the sweetness of rest and calm".

Therefore God really honors us, when he sets us in places where we must struggle. He is then giving us an opportunity to win the best honors and the richest blessing. Yet he never makes life so hard for us, in any circumstances, that we cannot live victoriously through the help which he is ready to give.

This lesson applies to **temptation**. Not one of us can miss being tempted—but we need never *fail* nor *fall* in it. Never yet was a child of God in any terrible conflict with the Evil One, in which it was not possible for him to overcome. There is a wonderful word in one of Paul's Epistles, which we should write in *letters of gold* on our chamber walls: "No temptation has overtaken you except what is common to humanity. God is faithful and He will not allow you to be tempted beyond what you are able, but with the temptation He will also provide a way of escape, so that you are able to endure it."

These are sublime assurances. Not one need ever say, "I *cannot* endure this temptation, and *must* yield and fall." This is never true. We need never fail. Christ met the sorest temptations—but he was always victorious; and now this tried and all-conquering Christ is by our side as we meet and endure our temptations, and we cannot fail when he is with us. It is possible, too, for us to so the meet temptations, as to change them into blessings. A conquered sin becomes a new strength in our life. We are stronger because every conquest gives us a new spirit of life; the strength we have defeated becomes now part of our own power.

Victoriousness in speech is among the hardest of life's conquests. The words of James are true to common experience, when he says that the tongue is harder to tame than any kind of beast or birds or creeping things or things in the sea; indeed, that no man can tame it. Yet he does not say that we need not try to tame our tongue. On the other hand he counsels us to be slow to speak and slow to anger. A Christian ought to learn to control his speech. The capacity for harm in angry words, is appalling. No prayer should be oftener on our lips than that in the old psalm, "Set a guard over my mouth, O Lord; keep watch over the door of my lips."

The hasty word in an uncontrolled moment—may leave sore wounding and pain in a gentle heart, may mar a sweet friendship, may set an innocent life on a career of evil. Also, the hurt in him who speaks ungoverned words, is scarcely less sore. The pain that quickly follows their utterance, is terrible penalty for the sin. There is ofttimes a cost, too, in results, which is incalculable. Lives have been shadowed, down to their close, by words which fell in a single flash from unlocked lips! Moses was not the only man who has been shut out of a land of promise—by reason of one unadvised word. It is better to suffer wrong in silence—than to run the risk of speaking in the excitement of anger.

One writes: "A single word spoken under the influence of passion, or rashly and inconsiderately spoken, may prove a source of abiding pain and regret. But the suffering of an act of injustice, of wrong, or of unkindness, in a spirit of meekness and forbearance, never renders us unhappy. The remembrance of a sinful or even a hasty word, is not infrequently the cause of very deep mortification. The reflection that our words manifested a weakness, if not a lack of moral and spiritual balance, humiliates us. It is a wound to our self-respect, and the consciousness that the regret is now unavailing adds a sting to the pain. But in the feeling that in our exercise of the meekness and forbearance inspired by the love of Christ we went further than we were bound to go, is not often a cause of distress. In a review of the act—we do not feel that we wronged ourselves by making too large a sacrifice, or that our failure to resent the injury and to attempt to retaliate was a mistake. Reason and conscience approve the course, and it is a source of satisfaction and comfort."

The lesson applies also to whatever in our environment makes life hard. Sometimes we find ourselves in places and conditions of living, in which it seems impossible for us to grow into strength and beauty of character. This is true of many young people in the circumstances in which they are born—and in which they must grow up. They find about them the *limitations of poverty*. They cannot get the education they seem to need—to fit them for anything better than the most ordinary career. They envy other young people who have so much better opportunities. But these limitations, which seem to make fine attainments impossible, ofttimes prove the very blessings through which nobleness is reached. *Early hardship* is the best school for training men. Not many of those who have risen to the best and truest success, began in easy places.

Sometimes it is *poor health* which appears to make it impossible for one to live grandly, at least to do much in the world. But this is not an insuperable barrier. Many people who have been invalids all their life, have grown into rare sweetness of spirit, and have lived in the world in a way to make it better, and to leave influences of blessing behind them when they went away. Many a "shut in " has made a narrow room and a *chamber of pain*—the center of a heavenly life, whose blessings have gone far and wide. At least, there is no condition of health in which one cannot live victoriously in one's spirit, if not physically. One can be brave, cheerful, accepting one's limitations, praising God in sickness and in pain, sure always that what God wills is best, and that he who sings his little song of joy and praise in his prison—is pleasing God and blessing the world.

Sometimes that which makes life hard is in one's own *temperament*. Passions are strong; temper seems uncontrollable; the affections are embittered, so that meekness and gentleness appear to be impossible; or the disposition is soured so that one finds it hard to be loving and sweet. The fault may be in one's early training, or the unhappy temper may be inherent. None of us come into the world saints, and ofttimes there are tendencies in one's childhood home, or in one's early years which give the wrong *bias* to the life. A few years later one awakes to find the nature misshapen, distorted, with the unlovely elements prominent and dominant.

Must one necessarily go through life to the end thus marred, with disposition spoiled, quick tempered, with appetites and passions uncontrollable? Not at all. In all these things we may be "more than conquerors through Him that loved us." The grace of Christ can take the most unlovely life—and change it into beauty. Godliness is impossible to none, where the grace of God is allowed to work freely and thoroughly.

Many people find in their own homes the greatest obstacle in the way of their becoming beautiful and gentle in life. Home ought to be the best place in the world in which to grow into Christlikeness. There all the influences, should be inspiring and helpful. It ought to be easy to be sweet in home's sacredness. Everything good ought there to find encouragement and stimulus. All home training should be towards "whatever things are lovely." *Home should be life's best school.* What the conservatory is to the little plant or flower which finds warmth, good soil, and gently culture there, growing into sweet loveliness; home should be to the young life that is born into it, and grows up within its doors. But not all home-life is ideal. Not in all homes, is it easy to live sweetly and beautifully. Sometimes the atmosphere is unfriendly, cold, cheerless, chilling. It is hard to keep the heart gently and kindly in the bitterness which creeps into home-life.

But no matter how sadly a home may fail in its love and helpfulness, how much there may be in it of sharpness and bitterness, it is the mission of a Christian always to be sweet, to seek to overcome the hardness, to live victoriously. This is possible, too—through the help of Christ.

These are only illustrations of this lesson. Many of us find ourselves in *uncongenial conditions* in which we must stay, at least for the time. But, whatever the circumstances, we may live Christianly. God will never allow us to be put in any place in which, though the help of his grace—we cannot be godly and beautiful Christians. *Limitations*, if we rightly use them, only help to make our life more earnest, more beautiful. A writer calls attention to the fact that every musical string is musical, because it is tied at both ends and must vibrate in limited measure of distance. Cut the string, and let it fly loose, and it no more gives out musical notes. Its musicalness depends upon its limitations. So it is with many human lives; they become capable of giving out sweet notes, only when they are compelled to move in restraint. The very hardness in their condition, is that which brings out the best qualities in them, and produces the finest results in character and achievement.

This lesson applies also to experiences of misfortune, adversity, or sorrow. Paul speaks of himself in one place as "sorrowful—yet always rejoicing." His *life* could not be crushed, his *joy* could not be quenched, his *songs* could not be hushed. We must all meet trial in some form—but one need never be overwhelmed by it. Yet it is very important that we should learn to pass through our sorrow as Christians. Do we meet it victoriously? We cannot help weeping; Jesus wept, and tears are sacred when love for our friends and love for Christ mingle in them. But our tears must not be rebellious. "May Your will be done" must breathe through all our sobbings and cries, like the melody of a sweet song in a dark night of storm.

Sorrow hurts some lives. It embitters them. It leaves them broken, disheartened, not caring more for life. But this is not the *Christian* way. We should accept sorrow, however it may come to us, as bringing with it a fragment of God's sweet will for us, as bringing also some new revealing of divine love. We should meet it quietly, reverently, careful not to miss the blessing it brings to us. Then we should rise up again at once, and go on with our work and duty. Some hands are left hanging down after grief has come. "I do not care any more for life," men are sometimes heard to say. "I have no interest in my business, since my wife died. I want to give it all up." But that is not victorious living. *Sorrow* absolves us from no duty, from no responsibility. Our work is not finished because our friend's work is done. God's plan for our life goes on—though for the life dearest to us, it has ended. We rise the morning after the funeral, and find the old tasks waiting for us, clamoring for our coming, and must go forth at once to take them up. "Let us dry our tears and go on," wrote a godly man to his friend, after a sore bereavement. That is the true Christian spirit.

We ought to live more earnestly than ever, after grief has touched our heart. Our life has been enriched by the experience. Tears leave the *soil of the heart* more fertile. The experience of sorrow teaches us many lessons. We are wiser afterward, more thoughtful, better fitted to be a guide and helper to others, and prepared especially to be comforters of those whom we find passing through affliction. Instead, therefore, of letting our hands hang down in despairing weakness, we should rise up quickly, fresh from our new anointing, and hasten on to the duty which waits for us.

Thus all Christian life should be victorious. We should never allow ourselves to be defeated, in any experience which may come to us. With Christ to help us, we need never fail—but may ever be more than conquerors. Even the things which seem to be failures and defeats in our lives—through the love and grace of Christ—if only we are faithful—will prove in the end to be successes and victories. Many a good man fails in a worldly sense, and yet in the moral and spiritual realm is more than conqueror. There is no real failure—but in sin. Faithfulness to Christ is victory, even when all is lost!

The Strength of Quietness

"Your beauty should not come from outward adornment, such as braided hair and the wearing of gold jewelry and fine clothes. Instead, it should be that of your inner self, **the unfading beauty of a gentle and quiet spirit**, which is of great worth in God's sight." 1 Peter 3:3-4

The Bible says a great deal about being quiet. The effect of righteousness, is quietness. The Shepherd leads His sheep by the waters of quietness. We are told to *"study to be quiet,"* or to *be ambitious to be quiet,* as a marginal reading gives it. A quiet spirit in a woman is, in Gods sight—an ornament of great price. Then we are told that a secret of strength lies in quietness, "In*quietness* and trust is your *strength.*" Isaiah 30:15.

So when we look into the matter, we learn that few things are so greatly praised or are so repeatedly encouraged in the Bible, as *quietness.* Quietness is a *result*—rather than a *means.* It indicates an attainment in the Christian life which can he reached only through certain spiritual experiences.

A deep truth lies here. Many people suppose that *noise* indicates *strength*; that the loud bombastic man is the strong one; that we are doing the most—when we make the most bluster and show. But this is not true.

In all of life, it is the *quiet forces* that have the greatest effect. The *sunbeams* fall silently all the day—yet what immeasurable energy there is in them, and what power for blessing and good!*Gravitation* is a silent force, with no rattle of machinery, no noise of engines—and yet it holds all the stars and worlds in perfect orbit with its invisible chains! The *dew* falls silently at night when men sleep—and yet it touches every plant and leaf and flower with new life and beauty.

So it is in the calm, quiet life—that the greatest strength is found. The power that is blessing the world these days, comes from the purity and sweetness of gentle mother-love; from the quiet influence of example in faithful fathers; from the patience and unselfishness of devoted sisters; from the tender beauty of innocent child-life in homes; above all, from the *silent cross*—and the divine Spirit's breathings of gentle stillness. The noiseless agencies are doing the most to bless the world. There is strength in quietness.

If therefore we want to be *strong*—we must learn to be *quiet.* A noisy talker is always weak. Quietness in speech, is a mark of self-mastery. The tendency of the grace of Christ in the heart—is to *soften* and *refine* the whole nature. It makes the very *tones of the voice* more gentle. It curbs *boisterousness* into *quietness.* It represses angry feelings—and softens them into the gentleness of love. It restrains resentments, teaching us to return kindness for unkindness, gentleness for rudeness, blessing for cursing, prayer for scorn and defiance. "Love is patient, love is kind. It does not envy, it does not boast, it is not proud. It is not rude, it is not self-seeking, it is not easily angered, it keeps no record of wrongs. Love does not delight in evil but rejoices with the truth. It always protects, always trusts, always hopes, always perseveres." (1 Corinthians 13:4-7).

The love of Christ in the heart—makes one like Christ, for He was quiet. He was never flustered. He never fumed or fussed. He was never anxious or worried. He never spoke impatiently. His voice was never heard on the street. There was a calmness in His soul that showed itself in every word He spoke, in all His bearing.

We will do well to learn this *lesson of quietness*. It will keep us from outbursts of temper, and from saying the rash and hasty words, which an hour later we are sorry for saying, and which often make so much bitterness and trouble for us. It will enable us to be cheerful and patient amid all the cares and vexations of life.

Quietness is a *blessed secret for wives and mothers* in a home. It is impossible for any woman, even though her household life is ideally Christian and happy—to avoid having experiences which try her sensitive spirit. Probably the most perfect marriage, has its harsh incidents and its rude contacts, which tend to disturb a wife and give her heartache. It is hard for a man to learn to be so gentle—that no *word* or *touch* or *act* or *habit* or *disposition* of his—shall ever hurt the heart of the woman he loves. Nothing but a love which is patient, and kind, and not self-seeking, and not easily angered—can be silent and *sweet*—not silent and *sullen*—in any circumstances, can make even holiest wedded life what it should be. Blessed is the wife who has learned this lesson!

Every home, with its parents and children, presents problems which only *quietness* can solve. *Tastes* differ. *Individuality* is often strong. There are almost sure to be self-assertive spirits, in even the smallest family, those who want their own way, who are not disposed to do even their fair share of yielding. In some homes, there are despotic spirits. In the best, there are *diversities* of spirit, and the process of self-discipline and training, requires years before all the household can dwell together in *ideal sweetness*.

A German musician, with an ear exquisitely sensitive to harmony, soon after arriving in our country, visited a local church. But the singing was badly out of tune—jarring his nerves painfully. He could not courteously leave, and so resolved to endure the *torture* as patiently as possible. Soon he distinguished amid the discord one voice, the soft clear voice of a woman, singing calmly, steadily, and in perfect tune. She was not disturbed by the noisy voices of **her** companions—but sang on patiently and sweetly. And as he listened, one voice after another was drawn by her gentle influence into harmony, until the whole congregation was singing in perfect tune.

So it often is—in the making of a home. At first the *individual lives* are self-assertive, and there is discord in the household. It takes time and patient love—to bring all into harmony. But if the wife and mother, the real homemaker, has learned this blessed lesson of quietness; her life is the one calm, clear, true song—which never falters, and which brings all the other lives, little by little, up to its own sweet key, until at last—the life of the home is indeed a song of love!

Sometimes it is a daughter and sister in the home, whose quiet sweetness blesses the whole household. She has learned the *lesson of patience and gentleness*. She has smiles for everyone. She has the *joyful tact* to dissipate little quarrels, by her kind words. She softens the father's ill-temper when he comes in weary from the day's cares. She is a peacemaker in the home, a happiness-maker, through the influence of her own lovingness of spirit—and draws all into her own quietness and peacefulness.

These are familiar illustrations of the *blessing of quietness*. Wherever we find it in any life, it has a wonder-working influence. It surely is a lesson worth learning—which is better than the winning of a crown! But can it be learned? Can the blustering, quick-tempered, rash-speaking man or woman—learn to be quiet and self-mastered? Yes! *Moses* learned it, until he became the meekest of men. *John* learned it, until he became the beloved disciple, lying on Jesus' bosom. It can be learned by anyone who will *enter Christ's school*, for He says, "Come unto Me. Take My yoke upon you and *learn of Me*; and you shall find rest unto your souls." (Matthew 11:28, 29).

But quietness never can come through the *smoothing of circumstances*, so that there shall be nothing to trouble or irritate the spirit. We cannot *find* or *make* a quiet place to live in—and *thus* get quiet in our own soul. We cannot make the people about us so loving and sweet—that we shall never have anything to irritate or annoy us. The quietness must be *within* us. Nothing but the peace of God in the heart—can give it. Yet we can have this peace—if we will simply and always do God's will—and then trust Him. A quiet heart—will give a quiet life!

The Blessing of Patience

"May the Lord direct Your hearts into the love of God, and into the *patience of Christ*." 2 Thessalonians 3:5

This is a *blessing* which all of us would like to bow our heads to receive. "Patience among the virtues," says one, "is like the *pearl* among the gems. By its *quiet radiance* it brightens every human grace and adorns every Christian excellence."

In Christ, patience, like all virtues, had its *perfection*. And His was not a *sheltered* life, without such trials of patience as we must endure—but one exposed to all that makes it hard for us to live patiently. Besides, His nature was one that was *sensitive to all rudeness and pain*—so that He suffered in His contacts with life far more than we do.

Yet His patience was perfect. "He came unto His own, and His own received Him not." He pressed upon them the gifts of love—but they rejected them. Yet He never failed in His loving, never grew impatient, never wearied in His offers of blessings, never withdrew His gracious gifts. He stood with His hands outstretched toward them—until they nailed those hands on the cross! And even then He let drop out of those pierced hands—the gift of redemption!

His patience appears also in His *dealings with His own disciples*. They were very ignorant and learned slowly. They tried Him at every point by their lack of faith, their lack of spirituality, and their weak, faltering friendship. But He never wearied in His love nor in His teaching.

His patience is seen in His treatment of the *people* who pressed about Him wherever He went, with their begging for healing. We have only to think what an Oriental crowd is, and then remember that it was the very *wreckage of misery and wretchedness*, that came to Him, to get a thought of the wearisomeness of moving day after day amid the clamors and cries of these poor sufferers. Yet He never showed the slightest impatience—but gave out freely and lovingly of the richest and best of His own precious life to heal and comfort them.

His patience with His *enemies* is also astonishing. It was not the patience of *weakness*, for at any moment He might have summoned legions of angels from heaven to strike down His opponents. Nor was it the patience of *stoicism,* that did not feel the stings of hate and persecution; for never was there another life on earth that felt so *keenly* the hurts of enmity. Nor was it the patience of *sullenness*, such as is sometimes seen in savages, who bear torture in grim, haughty silence.

Never did the world see any other patience, so loving. He prayed for His murderers! He gave back the most gentle answers—to the most cruel words. His response to the world's enmity—was the gift of salvation. From the cruel wounds made by nail and spear—came the blood of human redemption!

We see His patience also in His *work*. He saw very few results from His preaching. He was a sower, not a reaper. Multitudes flocked after Him, heard His words, and went away unimpressed.

Thus to whatever phase of Christ's wonderful life we turn—we see *sublime patience*. He was patient in accepting His Father's will; patient toward the world's sin and sorrow; patient with men's unreasonableness, unkindness and hatred; patient with ignorance and prejudice; patient in suffering wrong. Marvelous, indeed, is this quality in our Lord's life. Who is not ready to turn the blessing, into the prayer, "Lord, direct my heart into the patience of Christ."

We all need patience. Without it we never really can make anything of our lives. We need it in our *homes*. The very closeness and familiarity of the family members within our own doors—make it hard at times for us to preserve *perfect sweetness* of spirit. There is much lack of patience, in most earthly families. We throw off our reserve and our carefulness, and are apt to speak or act disagreeably. It is easy in the *friction* that too often is felt in our homes—to lose our patience and speak unadvisedly and unkindly. Such *impatient words* hurt gentle hearts, sometimes irreparably. But wherever else we may fail in patience—it should not be in our own homes! Only the *sweetest life* should be lived there. We have not long to stay together—and we should be patient and gentle while we may!

We need the patience of Christ also, in our mingling with others, in our *business* associations and contacts, in our *social* relations, and in all our dealings with our *neighbors*. Not all people are congenial and patient to us. Some want their own way. Some are unreasonable. Some fail to treat us right. Possibly in some cases—the fault may be ours, at least in part. Others may sometimes think of us—as we do of them. However this may be, the patience of Christ may teach us to bear with even the most unreasonable people, sweetly and lovingly. He was patient with everyone, and we are to be like Him. If we are impatient with anyone, we fail to he true to the interest of our Master, whom we are always to represent.

We need the patience of Christ in meeting the trials of life. We need only remember how sweetly He endured all wrongs, all pain and suffering—to get a vision of a very *beautiful ideal* of life to follow. The lesson is hard to learn—but the Lord can direct our hearts even into this gentleness of spirit. He can help us to be silent in the time of distress. He can turn our *cry of pain*—into a *song of submission and joy*. He can give us His steadfast peace, so that even in the wildest strife—our heart shall be quiet.

We need the patience of Christ—to prepare us for His service. The moment we enter the company of His disciples, He gives us work to do for Him. We are sent to find other souls, to bind up broken hearts, to comfort sorrow, to help lost ones find home through the gloom. All this work is *delicate* and important, and for it we need the *patience* as well as the *gentleness* of Christ. It must be done lovingly, in faith, unhurriedly, under the Spirit's guidance.

Mothers need the lesson of patience, that they may wisely teach and train their children, and not hurt their lives by impatience. All who are dealing with the *ignorant* need it. Those who would put their hands in any way on other lives— need a large measure of the patience of Christ. We must seek to do Christ's work for them—as He would do it if He were here—with those *gentle hands* of His. We need His patience also in *waiting*, as we work for God. We are in danger continually, in our very interest in others, of speaking inopportunely. Even eager, loving words— must wait for the *perfect time* for speaking them, or else they may do harm. Even in our hunger—*we must not pluck the fruit while it is yet unripe.*

As it is in Heaven

"May Your will be done on earth—*as it is in heaven.*" Matthew 6:10

"As it is in heaven" is the standard which the Lord's Prayer sets for us—in *doing God's will on earth*. It is a high ideal, and yet it cannot be no lower. The petition is a prayer that *heaven* may begin in our hearts here on the earth.

When a child was looking thoughtfully up into the depths of an evening sky, and wondering how one could get to heaven, as it seemed so far away and he could see no ladder, he was told by his wise mother, "Heaven must first come down into your heart." We must not forget this. We can never enter heaven—until heaven has entered into us. We must have the life of God in us—before we are ready to dwell in blessedness with God.

We forget that heaven is not *far off yonder*—but begins right here in our everyday lives, if it is ever to begin at all for us! Isn't that what the prayer means, "May Your will be done on earth—as it is in heaven"? "On earth," that is—in our shops, and our drudgery, and care; in our times of temptation and sorrow. It is not a prayer to be taken away out of this world into 'heaven', to begin*there* the doing of God's will; it is a prayer that *right here and now on earth*—we may learn to live—as they do in heaven.

How do they live in heaven? There all wills are in *perfect accord* with the divine will. We begin our Christian lives on earth, with hearts and wills much attune to our *old* nature. Naturally we want our own way—not God's. The beginning of the new life—is the acceptance of Christ as our King. But not at *once,* does the kingdom in us become fully His. It has to be subdued. Christian growth is simply—the bringing of our wills into perfect accord with God's. It is learning to do always the things that please God.

"Our wills are ours." But this is only half the truth. They are ours to give to God, to yield to His will. This is the whole work of Christian growth, of spiritual culture. We begin making our wills God's—when we first begin to follow Christ. But it takes all life to make the *surrender complete.* But taught of God, and helped by the divine Spirit—we come every day a little nearer doing God's will on earth—as it is done in heaven—if we are faithful.

"May Your will be done on earth." That means obedience, not partial—but full and complete obedience. It is taking the Word of God into our heart, and conforming our whole lives to it. It is accepting God's way always—sweetly and submissively—with love and faith.

The divine law is summed up in one word—*LOVE.* "You shall love." God is love. "As it is in heaven" means *love shining out in a pure, beautiful, holy life.* "May Your will be done on earth" means, therefore, *love.* All the lessons may be gathered into one—*learning to love.* Loving *God* is first. Then loving God begets in us—love to *all men.*

Do we understand what love is? Don't we usually think only of its earthly side? We like to be loved, that is, to have other people love us and live for us, and do things for us. We like the gratifications of love. But that is only *miserable selfishness*, if it goes no further. It is a desecration of the sacred name of love—to think that, at its heart, it means only getting, receiving. No, love GIVES. Getting is earthly; "as it is in heaven" is giving. That is what God's love does—it finds its blessedness in giving. "God so loved the world—that He GAVE His only begotten Son" (John 3:16). That is what Christ's love does—it pours out its very life-blood, to the last drop. The essential meaning of love must always be *giving*, not receiving.

Perhaps our thought of the blessings of heaven, is often a selfish one—that it will be all enjoyment, all receiving. But even heaven will not be an eternity of self-gratification, or only the bliss of receiving. Even there, especially there, where all imperfections will be left behind—love must find its supreme blessedness in giving, in serving others, in pouring out into other lives. There it will forever be more blessed to *give* than to receive, to *serve* rather than to be served.

"On earth as it is in heaven" means therefore not merely the gratification of *being* loved—but the blessedness of *loving* others and *giving* out the richest and best of one's life for others. Sometimes we hear people sighing to have *friends*, to be *loved*. This is natural. We all hunger for love. But this craving may become unwholesome, even miserably morbid. A great deal more wholesome, is the desire to *give love*, to be a blessing to others, to pour out the heart in refreshing other weary hearts.

It is God's will that we should *love*; it may not always be God's will that we should *be* loved. It seems to be the mission of some in this world—to give and not receive. They are to shine in the darkness, burning up their own lives as the lamp burns oil—to be light to other souls. They are called to serve, to minister, to wear out their lives in giving light, comfort, and help to others—while none come to minister to them, to pour love's sweetness into their hearts, and to give them the daily bread of affection, cheer, and help.

In many homes we find such lives—a patient wife and mother; or a gentle, unselfish sister—blessing, caring for, serving, giving perpetually love's richest gifts; themselves meanwhile unloved, unserved, unrecognized, and unhelped. We are apt to pity such people—but couldn't it be, that they are nearer the *heavenly ideal of doing God's will*—than are some of those who sit in the sunshine of love, receiving, ministered unto—but not giving or serving?

Was it not so with our Lord Himself? He *loved* and *gave* and *blessed* many, at last giving His very life—but few came to give Him blessing and the encouragement of love in His own soul. It is more divine to *love*—than to *be* loved. At least, God's will for us is that we should love, pouring out our hearts' richest treasures upon others—not asking meanwhile for any return. Loving is its own best return and reward.

Thus "as it is in heaven" always shines before us, as the ideal of our earthly lives. It is not a vague, shadowy ideal, for it is simply the complete doing of God's will. *Perfect obedience* is heaven. Sometimes it is serving others; sometimes it is quiet, patient suffering, or passive waiting. The one great lesson to be learned—is perfect accord with the will of God for us every moment, whatever that will may be.

"As it is in heaven" may seem far above us today. We say that the song is too *melodious*, for our unmusical voices to sing. We say that the life is too *ideal* for us, with our little faith.

But if only we are true to our Father's will; if only we keep our hearts always open to the love of Christ; and to the help and sanctifying influence of the Holy Spirit— we shall rise day by day toward heaven's perfection, until at last we shall enter the gates of peace and be *with* Christ and be *like* Him! For the present, our effort and our prayer should continually be: "May Your will be done on earth—**in us**—as it is done in heaven."

The *Shadows* We Cast

"For none of us *lives* to himself, and no one dies to himself." Romans 14:7

Every one of us casts *a shadow*. There hangs about us, a sort *of a strange, indefinable something,* which we call *personal influence*—that has its effect on every other life on which it falls. It goes with us wherever we go. It is not something we can have when we want to have it, and then lay aside when we will, as we lay aside a garment. It is something that always pours out from our lives, as light from a lamp, as heat from flame, as perfume from a flower.

The *ministry of personal influence* is something very wonderful. Without being conscious of it, we are always impressing others by this *strange power* that exudes from us. Others watch us—and their thinking and actions are modified by our influence. Many a life has been started on a career of beauty and blessing—by the influence of a noble act. The disciples saw their Master praying, and were so impressed by His earnestness or by the radiance they saw on His face as He communed with His Father, that when He joined them again—they asked Him to teach them how to pray. Every sincere person is continually impressed by the glimpses he has of loveliness, of holiness, or of nobleness in others. One kind deed often inspires others to act in a kinder way.

Here is a story from a newspaper which illustrates this. A little newsboy entered a subway train, and dropping into a seat was soon asleep. At the next stop two young ladies came in and took seats opposite to him. The child's feet were bare, his clothes were ragged, and his face was pinched and drawn, showing marks of hunger and suffering. The young ladies noticed him, and seeing that his cheek rested against the hard window-sill, one of them arose and quietly raising his head, slipped her folded scarf under it for a pillow.

The kind act was observed, and now mark its influence. An old gentleman in the next seat, without a word, held out a quarter to the young lady, nodding toward the boy. After a moment's hesitation she took it, and as she did so, another man handed her a dime, a woman across the aisle held out some pennies and almost before the young woman realized what she was doing, she was *taking a collection,* everyone in the car passing her something for the poor boy. Thus from the young woman's one gentle little act—there had gone out a wave of influence touching the hearts of almost forty people, and leading each of them to do something.

Common life is full of just such illustrations of the influence of kind deeds. Every godly life leaves a *twofold ministry* in this world: that of the things it does directly to bless others; and that of the silent influence it exerts, through which others are made better, or inspired to do like good things.

Influence is something, too, which even death does not end. When earthly life closes, a godly man's work ceases. He is missed in the places where his familiar presence has brought blessings. No more are his words heard by those who have many times been cheered or comforted by them. No more do his benefactions find their way to homes of need where so often they have brought relief. No more does his loving friendship minister strength or hope or courage to hearts that have learned to love him. The death of a godly man in the midst of his usefulness, cuts off a blessed ministry of helpfulness in the circle in which he has lived. But his *influence* continues!

The influence which our dead have over us—is frequently very great. We think we have *lost* them—when we see their faces no more, nor hear their voices, nor receive the accustomed kindness at their hands. But in many cases, there is no doubt that what our loved ones do for us after they are gone—is quite as important as what they could have done for us had they stayed with us. The *memory of beautiful lives* is a blessing, softened and made more rich and impressive, by the sorrow which their departure caused. The influence of such *sacred memories* is in a certain sense, more tender than that of life itself. Death *transfigures* our loved one, as it were, sweeping away the *faults* and *blemishes* of the mortal life—and leaving us an abiding vision in which all that was *beautiful* and *pure* and *gentle* and *true* in him, remains to us.

We often lose friends in the competitions and strife of earthly life, whom we would have kept forever had death taken them away in the earlier days, when love was strong. Often is it true, "He lives to us—who dies; but he is lost—who lives." Thus even death does not quench the *influence of a godly life*. It continues to bless others—long after the life has passed from earth.

Therefore, we need to guard our influence with most conscientious care. It is a crime to carry contagion to men's homes. It is a worse crime to send out a printed page bearing words infected with the virus of moral death. The men who prepare and publish the vile literature which today goes everywhere polluting and defiling innocent lives, will have a dreadful account to render when they stand at God's bar to meet their influence. If we would make our lives worthy of God and a blessing to the world—we must see to it that nothing we do shall influence others to do evil in the slightest degree.

In the early days of American art, there went from the States to London, a young artist of genius and of a pure heart. He was poor—but had an inspiration for a holy life, as well as fine painting. Among his pictures was one that in itself was pure, but that by a sensuous mind might possibly be interpreted in an evil way. A lover of art saw this picture and purchased it. But when it was gone the young artist began to think of its possible *damaging influence*, and his conscience troubled him. He went to the buyer and said: "I have come to buy back my picture." The purchaser could not understand him. "Didn't I pay you enough for it? Do you want more money?" he asked. "I am poor," replied the artist, "but my art is my life. Its mission must be holy. The influence of that picture may possibly be harmful. I cannot be happy with it before the eyes of the world. It must be withdrawn."

We should keep watch over our words and deeds—not only in their intent and purpose—but also in their *possible influence* over others. There may be *liberties* which in us lead to no danger—but which to others with a less stable character, and less helpful environment, would be full of peril. It is part of our duty to think of these *weaker ones* and of the *influence* of our example upon them. We may not do anything in our spiritual strength and liberty, which might possibly harm others. We must be willing to sacrifice our liberty—if by its exercise, we endanger another's soul. This is the teaching of Paul in the words: "It is a noble thing not to eat meat, or drink wine, or do anything that makes your brother stumble" (Romans 14:21). "Therefore, if what I eat causes my brother to fall into sin, I will never eat meat again, so that I will not cause him to fall" (1 Cor. 8:13).

How can we make sure, that *our influence* shall be only a blessing? There is no way—but by making our lives pure and holy. Just in the measure that we are filled with the Spirit of God, and have the love of Christ in us—shall *our influence* be holy and a blessing to the world. "Be very careful, then, how you live—not as unwise but as wise, making the most of every opportunity." Ephesians 5:15-16

On the Bearing of Our Burden

"Come to Me, all of you who are weary and burdened, and I will give you rest. All of you, take up My yoke and learn from Me, because I am gentle and humble in heart, and you will find rest for yourselves. For My yoke is easy and My burden is light." Matthew 11:28-30

We all have our burdens. Of course, they are not the same in all. Some are more apparent than others. There are people whose burdens we all *see.* These get our sympathy; we come up to them with love's warmth and help. There are others, however, whose burdens are *not visible.* It seems to us they have no trouble, no struggle, no loads to carry. We envy their lot. Probably, however, if we knew all that God knows about their lot—our *envy* would change to *sympathy.* The burdens that the world cannot see—are often the heaviest. The sorrows that are not announced in the obituaries, and endure no *viewing*—are often the hardest to bear.

It is not wise for us to think that our burden is greater than our neighbor's; perhaps his is really greater than ours. We sometimes wish that we might change places with some other person. We imagine that our lives would he a great deal easier, if we could do this, and that we could live more amiably and beautifully than we do, or more usefully and helpfully.

But if we really did change places with the one who, for all we know, seems to us to have the most favored lot; if we really did take this person's place, with all its conditions, its circumstances, its responsibilities, its cares, its duties, its blessings—there is little doubt that we would quickly cry out to God to give us back our own old place, and our own burden! It is because we do not know everything about him, that we think our neighbor's load lighter and more easily borne, than our own.

There are three Bible words about the bearing of burdens. One tells us that *"Every man shall bear his own burden"* (Gal. 6:5). There are burdens that no one can carry for us—not even Christ; burdens that no one can even share. This is true in a very real sense of life itself, of duty, of one's relation to God, of one's personal responsibility. No one can live your life for you. Friends may help you by encouragement, by sympathy, by counsel, by guidance—but, after all, in the innermost meaning of your life—you must live it yourself. No one can make your decisions for you. No one can have faith in God for you. No one can obey the commandments for you. No one can get your sins forgiven for you. No one can do your duties or meet your responsibilities for you. No one can take your place in any of the great experiences of life. A friend might be willing to do it—but it is simply impossible. *David* would have died for *Absalom*—he loved his son well enough to do this, but he could not do it. Many a mother would take her child's burden of pain, as she sees it in anguish—and bear it for the child—but she can only sit beside it and watch it suffer; she cannot take its place. Everyone must live his own life.

There is another Bible word which tells us that we should *"bear one another's burdens"* (Gal. 6:2). So there are burdens which others *can* help us carry. No one can do our duty for us, or take our load of suffering—but human friendship can put *strength* into our heart to make us better able to do or to endure. It is a great thing to have brotherly help in life. We all need each other. Not one of us could carry on without others to *share his burdens*. And we begin to be like Christ—only when we begin to help others, to be of use to them, to make life a little easier for them, to give them some of our *strength* in their weakness, some of our *joy* in their sorrow. When we have learned this lesson—we have begun to live worthily.

There is another inspired word which tells us to *"cast your burden upon the Lord—and He will sustain you"* (Psalm 55:22). The word "burden" in this passage, in the margin of the King James Version, is rendered "gift". "Cast your *gift* upon the Lord." In the Revised Version, the marginal reading is, "Cast what He has *given* you upon the Lord." This is very suggestive. Our *burden* is that which God has *given* to us. It may be duty; it may be struggle and conflict; it may be sorrow; it may be our environment. But whatever it is—it is that which He has given us, and we may cast it upon the Lord.

The form of the promise is also suggestive. We are not told that the *Lord* will carry our burden for us, or that He will *remove* it from us. Many people infer that this is the meaning—but it is not. Since it is that which God has *given* to us—it is in some way *needful* for us. It is something under which we will best grow into spiritual strength and beauty. Our *burden* has a *blessing* in it for us. This is true of duty, of trials and temptations, of the things which to us seem hindrances, of our disappointments and sorrows; these are all ordained by God as the best means for the development of our lives. Hence it would not be a true kindness to us—for God to *take away* our burden, even at our most earnest pleading, It is part of our maturing. There is a blessing in the bearing of it.

The promise is, therefore, not that the Lord will *remove* the load we cast upon Him, nor that He will *carry* it for us—but that *He will sustain us so that we may carry it.* He does not *free* us from duty—but He *strengthens* us for it. He does not *deliver* us from conflict—but He *enables* us to overcome. He does not withhold or withdraw trial from us—but He helps us in trial to be submissive and victorious, and makes it a blessing to us. He does not mitigate the hardness or severity of our circumstances, taking away the uncongenial elements, removing the thorns, making life easy for us—but He puts into our hearts *divine grace*, so that we can live serenely in all the hard, adverse circumstances.

This is the law of all spiritual life—not the lifting away of the burden—but the giving of help to *enable us to carry it with joy.*

Much *human* love, in its shortsightedness, errs in always trying to *remove* the burden. Parents think they are showing true and wise affection to their children, when they make their tasks and duties easy for them—but really they may be doing them *irreparable harm*, dwarfing their lives and marring their future! So all tender friendship is apt to over-help and over-protect. It ministers relief, lifts away loads, gathers hindrances out of the way—when it would help far more wisely, by seeking rather to impart *hope, strength, courage.*

But God never makes this mistake with His children. He never fails us in need—but He loves us too much to relieve us of *weights* which we need to carry—to make our growth healthful and vigorous. He never over-helps. He wants us to grow strong, and therefore He trains us to strain, to struggle, to endure, to overcome; not heeding our requests for the *lightening* of the burdens—but, instead, putting into us *more grace* as the load grows heavier—that we may always live courageously and victoriously!

This is the secret of the peace of many a *sickroom*, where one sees always a smile on the face of the weary sufferer. The pain is not taken away—but the power of Christ is given, and the suffering is endured with patience. It is the secret of the deep, quiet joy we frequently see in the Christian *home of sorrow*. The grief is crushing—but God's blessed comfort comes in gentle whispers, and the mourner rejoices. The grief is not taken away. The dead are not restored. But the divine love comes into the heart, making it strong to accept the sorrow and say, "May Your will be done!" (Matthew 6:10)

Judging Others

One of our Lord's counsels to his followers is, "Judge not, that you be not judged."

We cannot judge others fairly. For example, we do not know what may be the *causes* of the faults we would condemn in others.

Some people's infirmities are *hereditary*. Or there may be something in their *circumstances* or *experiences,* which is the cause of the peculiarities we are disposed to censure. We do not know what *hidden troubles* people have — what *secret sorrows.*

Longfellow somewhere says, "If we could read the *secret history* of our enemies, we would find in each man's life, sorrow and suffering enough to disarm all hostility!" *If we knew all that God knows of people's lives, our censure would turn to pity!*

We are in danger of misjudging the acts and character of others, also, because we can see only a *fragment* of their life. There are two sides to most things and people, and we usually see but one.

One Christmas the poet Whittier received from a friend a flower pressed between two panes of glass. One side showed only a blurred mass of leaves and stems, without beauty. The other side revealed all the loveliness of the flower as it lay beneath the glass. Mr. Whittier hung his gift in his window, and turned the beautiful side inward. Those who passed outside saw only "a grey disk of clouded glass," and wondered that the poet hung such an unsightly thing in his window. But he, sitting within, saw all the exquisite loveliness of the flower. Other things besides pressed flowers have two sides, and Whittier writes:

"Deeper musings come to me,
My half-immortal flower, from thee;
Man judges from a *partial* view;
None ever yet his brother knew.

The *eternal Eye* that sees the whole
May better read the darkened soul,
And find to outward sense denied,
The flower upon its inmost side."

Too often we see only the *blurred side* of people — and most people have a blurred side. Behind their rough exterior, however, may be a true heart, gentle and kindly.

We know a man out in the world among men, and he seems harsh, stern, ungentle. But some day we see him at home where his sick child suffers, and there he is another man — thoughtful, patient, almost motherly. It would have been most unjust if we had made up our judgment of him from *the outside view* only.

A young man was severely criticized by his companions for his miserliness. He was receiving a good salary but lived in a pinched way, without even the plain comforts which he could easily have afforded — his fellow-clerks thought. He never spent a penny for luxuries and avoided the expenses which other young men thought necessary. That was *one side* of the young man's life, and there were those who judged him by it.

But there was another side. He had an only sister — they were orphans — who was a great sufferer. She was confined to her room and bed, a helpless invalid. This brother provided for her. That was the reason he lived so cheaply, saving and doing without things for himself. He made these personal sacrifices, that his sister in her loneliness and pain, might have comforts. That was the *other side* of the character, the one side of which had seemed so unattractive to the young man's friends.

There are countless cases of this kind. We see a person's *actions* and form an unfavorable opinion — not knowing the true motive or reason for the actions.

The Pharisees judged Jesus and condemned him bitterly for eating with publicans and sinners, and showing himself the friend of these outcast classes. They saw him only in the light of their own prejudice, and they inferred that he was not a godly man, or he would not have chosen such companions. But we know that he went among these despised and fallen ones, that he might save them. The judgment of his enemies was wrong, because it was passed upon only a *fragment* of the truth.

Our own imperfections also unfit us for judging fairly. One who has no art taste cannot be a fair critic of works of art. We with our marred and imperfect moral nature, cannot judge righteously of the work and character of another.

The very faults we condemn in our neighbors — oft-times exist in ourselves in even graver form! Jesus teaches this when he says, "Why do you behold the *mote* that is in your brother's eye — but do not consider the *beam* that is in your own eye?" While we are finding *little specks of fault* in others and judging and condemning them on account of these motes — we ourselves have greater faults! We are not fit to be judges of others, because we have the same faults which we see in them.

Besides, while we are looking after the faults of *others* — we are in danger of neglecting the care of *our own* life!

"You, then, why do you **judge** your brother? Or why do you look down on your brother? For we will all stand before God's judgment seat. So then, each of us will give an account of himself to God. Therefore let us stop passing judgment on one another. Instead, make up your mind not to put any stumbling block or obstacle in your brother's way." Romans 14:10-13

Other People

"So in everything, *do unto others*—what you would have them do unto you, for this sums up the Law and the Prophets." Matthew 7:12

There are *other people*. We are not the only ones. Some of the others live close to us, and some farther away. We have a certain relationship to these other people. They have claims upon us. We owe them duties, services, love. We cannot cut ourselves off from them, from any of them—and say they are nothing to us. We cannot rid ourselves of *obligations* to them—and say we owe them nothing. So inexorable is this relationship to others—that in all the broad earth, there is not an individual who has no right to come to us with his needs, claiming at our hand, the ministry of love. The other people are *our brothers*, and there is not one of them that we have a right to despise or neglect or thrust away from our door.

We ought to train ourselves—*to think of the other people.* We may not leave them out of any of the plans we make. They have rights as well as we do—and we must consider these in asserting our own. No man may set his fence a hairs-breadth over the line on his neighbor's ground. No man may gather even a head of his neighbor's wheat. No man may enter his neighbor's door unbidden. No man may do anything which will harm his neighbor. Other people have inalienable rights—which we may not invade.

We owe other people more than *their rights*; we owe them *love*. To some of them it is not hard to pay this debt. They are lovable and winsome. They are thoroughly respectable. They are congenial spirits, giving us in return quite as much as we can give them. It is natural to love them, and be very kind and gentle to them. But we have no liberty of *selection* in this broad duty of loving other people. If we claim to be Christians, we may not choose *whom* we will love.

The Master's teaching is inexorable: "If you love those who love you, what credit is that to you? Even 'sinners' love those who love them. And if you do good to those who are good to you, what credit is that to you? Even 'sinners' do that. And if you lend to those from whom you expect repayment, what credit is that to you? Even 'sinners' lend to 'sinners,' expecting to be repaid in full. But love your enemies, do good to them, and lend to them without expecting to get anything back. Then your reward will be great, and you will be sons of the Most High, because he is kind to the ungrateful and wicked." (Luke 6:32-35).

The *Good Samaritan* is our Lord's answer to the question, "Who is my neighbor?" and the Good Samaritan's neighbor was a bitter enemy, who, in other circumstances, would have spurned him from his presence. Other people may not be beautiful in their character, nor congenial in their habits, manners, modes of life, or disposition; they may even be unkind to us, unjust, unreasonable; in strict justice altogether undeserving of our favor; yet if we persist in being called *Christians* ourselves, we owe them the love that thinks no evil, that seeks not its own, that bears all things, endures all things, and never fails.

That is, we owe other people *service*. Serving goes with *loving*. We cannot love sincerely, and not serve. Love without serving is but an empty sentiment, a poor mockery. God so *loved* the world, that He *GAVE*. Love always gives. If it will not give—it is not love. It is measured always by what it will give. The needs of other people are, therefore, divine commands to us which we dare not disregard or disobey. To refuse to help a brother who stands before us in any kind of need, is as great a sin as to break one of the commandments of the Decalogue.

We like to think there is no sin in *merely not doing*. But Jesus, in His wonderful picture of the Last Judgment, makes men's condemnation, turn on *not doing the things which they ought to have done*. They have simply not fed the hungry, nor clothed the naked, nor visited the sick, nor blessed the prisoner. To make these *sins of neglect* appear still more grievous, our Lord makes a personal matter of each case, puts Himself in the place of the sufferer who needs it and is not cared for, and tells us that all neglect in giving needed kindness to any—is neglect shown to *Him*. This divine word gives a tremendous interest to *other people* who are brought providentially into the sphere of our lives, so that their needs of any kind, must appeal to our sympathy and kindness. To neglect *them*—is to neglect *Christ*.

This matter of *serving* has multitudinous forms. Sometimes it is poverty that stands at our gate, and financial help is needed. But a thousand times more frequently, it is not money—but something else more precious that we must give. It may be *loving sympathy*. Sorrow is before us. Another's heart is breaking. Money would be of no use; it would be only a bitter mockery. But we can hold to the sufferer's lips, a cup filled out of our own heart, which will give new strength. Or it is the *anguish of a life struggle*, a human Gethsemane, beside which we are called to watch. We can give no actual aid—the soul must fight its battles alone—but we can be as the angel in our Lord's Gethsemane, *imparting strength* and helping the weary struggler to win the victory.

The world is very full of sorrow and trial, and we cannot live among our fellow men and be true to Christ, without sharing their loads. *Selfishness* must die, or our own heart's life must be frozen within us. We begin to felicitate ourselves on some special prosperity, and the next moment some human need knocks at our door, and we must share our good things with a suffering brother. We may build up our *fine theories* of taking care of ourselves, of living for the future, of laying up in the summer of prosperity for the winter of adversity, of providing for old age or for our children—but often all these frugal and economic plans have to yield to the *exigencies of human need*. The love that seeks not its own—plays havoc with *life's hard logic*. We cannot say that anything is our own when our brother is suffering, from what we can give.

Not a day passes in the commonest experiences of life, in which other people do not stand before us with their needs, appealing to us for some service which we may render. It may be only ordinary courtesy, the gentle kindness of the home circle, the patient treatment of neighbors or customers in business relations, the thoughtful showing of interest in old people or in children. On all sides, the lives of other people touch ours—and we cannot do just as we please, thinking only of ourselves and our own comfort and good—unless we choose to be false to all the instincts of humanity, and all the requirements of the law of Christian love. We must think continually of other people. We may not seek our own pleasure in any way— without asking whether it will harm or impair the comfort of some other.

For example, we must think of other people's convenience, in the exercise of our own liberty, and in the indulgence of our own tastes and desires. It may be pleasant for us to lie late in bed in the morning, and we may be inclined to regard the habit as only *a little harmless self-indulgence.* But there is a more serious side to the practice. It breaks the harmonious flow of the household life. It causes confusion in the family plans for the day. It makes extra work for the wife or mother. It sorely tries the patience of love.

The other day an important committee of fifteen was kept waiting for ten minutes for one tardy member whose presence was necessary before anything could he done. At last he came sauntering in without even an apology for having caused fourteen busy men a loss of time that to them was very valuable, besides having put a strain on their patience and good nature. We have no right to forget or disregard the convenience of others. A conscientious application of the Golden Rule would cure us of all such carelessness.

These are but illustrations of the way other people impinge upon our lives. They are so close to us that we cannot move without touching them. We cannot speak without having our words affect others. We cannot act in the simplest thing— without first thinking whether what we are about to do will help or hurt others. We are but one of a great family, and we dare not live for ourselves. We must never forget, that *there are other people!*

Loving Your Neighbor

"You shall love your neighbor as yourself." Mark 12:31

Definitions are important. *Who* is my neighbor? *What* is it to love my neighbor? If we can make "neighbor" mean just a little set of people, our own set; and if we can define "love" to suit our own selfish notions, it will be comparatively easy to pray, "Lord, incline our hearts to keep this law." But Scripture does not yield itself to our interpretation in this way. We cannot take its words, as the potter takes the clay, and mold them to suit our pleasure. Both *neighbor* and *love* are clearly defined in the Bible.

It once happened that a certain man asked Jesus WHO his neighbor was, and we have the answer in the *parable of the Good Samaritan.* A neighbor is anyone who happens to be near us and is in any need, distress, or danger. He may be the worst man in the land, outlawed by his own sins; still if he is near to us and needs our help—he is our neighbor, the man the commandment bids us to love. We would be willing enough to love our neighbors, if we could choose them—but this we cannot do. We must let God choose the particular neighbor He wants us to love.

WHAT is it to love our neighbor? It is the *loving* that is hard. We could do almost anything else, short of loving unpleasant neighbors.

But love is the word, and no *revised version* changes it. No matter how disagreeable, unlovely, unworthy, our neighbors for the time may be, still the commandment persistently and relentlessly says to us, *"You shall love him!"*

Our neighbors are about us all the time, needing our love. Indeed, they touch our lives so continually, that we must guard our every look, word, and act—lest we hurt some sensitive spirit.

Some people seem to forget that *other people have feelings*. They are constantly saying words and doing things which give pain. True love is *thoughtful*. We ought to train our hearts to the *most delicate sense of kindness*, that we may never ever jokingly give pain to any other human being. Our neighbors have hearts, and we owe to every one of them—the beggar we meet on the street, the poor wretch we find crawling in the mire of sin's debasement, the enemy who flings his insults in our face—to everyone, we owe the love that is thoughtful, gentle, and gives no hurt.

We should train ourselves to such reverence, to such regard for human life, that we shall never injure the heart of one of God's creatures, even by a disdainful look.

Our love ought also to be *patient*. Our neighbor may have his faults. But we are taught to bear with one another's infirmities. If we knew the story of men's lives, the hidden burdens they are often carrying for others, the unhealed wound in their heart—we would have most gentle patience with them. Life is hard for most people, certainly hard enough without our adding to its burdens—by our criticisms, our jeering and contempt, and our lack of love.

The things love does NOT do, must also be considered. Many of us fail in our *neglect* of love's duty—quite as much as in the *wounds* we give to others. We walk in cold silence beside one whose heart is aching or breaking, not saying the warm, rich word of love we might say, and which would give so much comfort. All about us are hungry ones, and the Master is saying to us, "Give them something to eat!" (Mark 6:37). But we are withholding from them—what we might give; and they are starving—when they might be filled.

We do not mean to be neglectful. The fact is, we have no idea that we could be of such blessing to others, as we might be. We do not dream that with *our poor, coarse barley loaves*—we might feed thousands. We are too frugal with our *heart gifts*. God has given us love—that with it we may make life sweeter, better, easier, more victorious and joyful for others. We do a *grievous wrong* to those about us—when we are *stingy* with the measure of love we give them; when we withhold the words of cheer, appreciation, encouragement, affection, and comfort which are in our hearts to speak; or when we fail to do the gentle, kind things we could so easily do—to make life happier and more pleasant for them.

The lesson is of wide—and has the very widest application. It touches our relationships with all men. It touches the pushing of our business interests; in our ambition to get, we must not forget our neighbor. It touches our influence; we must not do that which will hurt our neighbor or cause him to stumble. It has its important bearing on missions; we owe love to the perishing ones far or near—to whom we may carry or send the gospel of salvation.

"Your neighbor" is any man, woman, or child, of whatever character, condition, nation, or religion, whom God may place near you in need.

But there is an *inner circle*. There is a *brotherhood in Christ* that is closer still. We are to do good to all men, *especially* to those who are of the household of faith. That does *not* mean, merely one's own particular church.

One who went up in a balloon said that as he arose, the fences that divided the country into fields and farms faded out, until soon he saw only one great, wide, beautiful landscape of meadow and field and forest, with winding stream and river, shining in rich loveliness beneath the pure skies. So it is, as we rise nearer to God in love and faith and Christian experience. The *fences that divide* God's great church into ecclesiastical farms and pasture fields, grow smaller and smaller, until at last they vanish altogether; and we see only one wide, holy, Christlike church. All true Christians are one in Christ. Most differences of denominationalism are but of minor importance, in comparison with the love of Christ, the cross, the Bible, and heaven—which all true Christians have in common. We should learn to love one another as Christians; love soon breaks down the fences. We should comfort one another and help one another, on the way home.

The Cost of Being a Friend

"We loved you so much that we were delighted to share with you not only the gospel of God—but our lives as well, because you had become so dear to us!" 1 Thessalonians 2:8

We use the word "friend" very lightly. We talk of our *dozens of friends*, meaning all with whom we have common friendly relations, or even pleasant acquaintance. We say a person is our friend—when we know him only in business, or socially, when his heart and ours have never touched in any real communion. There may be nothing amiss in this wide application of the word—but we ought to understand that used in this sense—its full sacred meaning is not even touched.

To become another's friend in the true sense—is to take the other into such close, living fellowship, that his life and ours are knit together as one. It is far more than a *pleasant companionship* in bright, sunny hours. It is more than an association for mutual interest or profit or enjoyment. A genuine friendship—is entirely unselfish. It seeks no benefit or good of its own. It does not love—for what it may *receive*—but for what it may *give*. Its aim is "not to be served—but to serve" (Mark 10:45).

It *costs* to be a friend. "For better, for worse, for richer, for poorer, in sickness and in health," runs all true friendships. When we take a person into our lives as a friend, we do not know what it may cost us to be faithful to our trust. Misfortune may befall our friend, and he may need our help in ways that will lay a heavy burden on us.

It may be in his business or in his secular affairs, that he may suffer. Timely aid may enable him to overcome his difficulties, and attain to prosperous circumstances. It may be in our power to render him the assistance he needs, without which he must succumb to failure. It will cost us personal *inconvenience* and *trouble* to do this. But he is our friend. We have taken him into our lives, thus becoming partner in all his affairs. Can we withhold from him the help which he needs and which we can give, without breaking the holy compact of friendship and failing in our sacred obligations to him?

It may be the *misfortune* of *sickness* and *broken health,* which falls upon our friend. He is no longer able to be helpful to us as he was in the days when the friendship was first formed. Then he could contribute his part in the mutual ministering, *giving* as well as *receiving.* Then friendship for him brought us no care, no anxiety; exacted from us, no self-denial, no sacrifice. Then friendship for him laid on us no load, no burden.

On the other hand, it *was* full of helpfulness. It brought strength to our heart by its loving cheer. It was a blessing to our lives, in its warm inspirations, in its sweet comfort, in its satisfying affection. It stood beside us in all our times of trial, with full sympathy, putting its shoulder under our burdens, aiding us by its counsel, its encouragement. It brought its countless benefits and gains. But *now* in its feeble and broken state, it can no longer give us this strong help and uplift. Instead, it has become a *burden.* We must carry the loads alone—which his friendship so generously shared. He needs our help now, and can give in return—only a weight of care.

For example, a *wife* becomes an *invalid.* In the early days of wedded life— she *was* her husband's true helpmeet, his loyal partner in all duty, care, work, and burden-bearing. Her friendship brought back far more than it cost. But *now* she can only lie still amid the cares, and see him meet them alone. Instead of *sharing* his burdens, she herself has become an *added* burden which he must carry! But his love doesn't falter for a moment. He loved her—not for the help she was to him—but for her own dear sake. Hence his love doesn't change when she is no longer a strong helpmeet—but a burden instead. His heart only grows more tender, his hand more gentle, his spirit braver. He finds even deeper, sweeter joy now in *serving* her—than he found before in *being served* by her.

That is the meaning of true friendship, wherever it exists. It is not based on any helpfulness or service which it must *receive,* as its condition. Its source is in the heart itself. Its essential desire is to *help* and *serve.* It makes no nice calculation of so much to be *given*—and so much to be *received.* It stops at no cost which faithfulness may entail. It hesitates at no self-denial which may be necessary in the fulfillment of its duties. It does not complain when everything has to be given up. It only grows *stronger* and more *faithful* and *loyal*—as the demands for giving and serving become larger.

There is another phase of the *cost of friendship* which must not be overlooked: that which comes with the revealing of *faults* and *flaws* and *sins*. We see people at first, only on the surface of their lives—and we begin to admire them. We are attracted to them by qualities that win our attention. As we become associated with them, we become interested in them. At length our affection goes out to them, and we call them *our friends*. We walk with them in pleasant companionship that makes no demands on our unselfishness, and that discloses but little of their inner life. We know them as yet, only on the *surface* of their character, having no real acquaintance with the *self* that is hidden behind *life's conventionalities*. Nothing has occurred in the progress of our friendship, to bring out the things in their disposition, which are not altogether lovely.

At length, *closer intimacy* or difficult circumstances, reveal their faults and blemishes. We learn that under the *attractive exterior* which so pleased us—there are sins, spots, flaws, shortcomings, which sadly disfigure the beauty of their life. We discover in them elements of selfishness, untruthfulness, deceitfulness, or evil, which pain us. We find that they have *secret habits* which are *repulsive*. There are things in their *disposition*, never suspected in the days of common social conversation, which show offensively in the *closer relations of friendship's intimacy*.

This is often so in *wedded* life; the longest and freest acquaintance previous to marriage, reveals only the *better* side of the life of both. But the same is true in a greater or lesser degree, in all close friendships.

Many times this is a severe test of love. It is only as we rise into something of the *spirit of Christ*, that we are able to meet this test of friendship. He takes us as we are—and does not weary of us, whatever faults and sins display themselves in us. There is infinite comfort in this for us. We are conscious of our *unworthiness* and of the *unloveliness* and *vileness* which are in our souls. There are things in our lives—which we would not reveal to the world. Many of us have *pages in our biography* which we would not dare to spread out before the eyes of men! There are in our inner being—evil feelings, desires, longings, cravings, jealousies, motives—which we would not feel secure in laying bare to our nearest, dearest, and most gentle and patient friend!

Yet Christ knows them all. Nothing is hidden, nothing *can* be hidden from His eyes. To Him there is a perfect revealing of the innermost recesses of our heart. Yet we need not be afraid that His friendship for us will change or grow less, or withdraw itself—when He discovers in us *repulsive things*. This is the ideal human friendship. It is not *repelled* by the *revealing of faults*. Even if the friend has fallen into sin—the love yet clings, forgiving and seeking his restoration.

We are apt to complain if our friends do not *return* as deep, rich, and constant a love—as we give them. We feel hurt at any evidence of the *ebbing* of love in them, when they *fail* us in some way, when we think they have not been altogether faithful and unselfish, or when they have been thoughtless or indifferent toward us. But

Christ saw in His own redeemed people—a very feeble return for all His deep love for them, a most inadequate requital for all His wondrous goodness and grace. They were unreliable, weak, unfaithful, sometimes inconsiderate and thoughtless. Yet He continued to love them in spite of all that He found unlovely and unworthy in them.

This is the friendship He would teach His disciples. As He loves us—He would have us love others. We say men are not worthy of such friendships. True, they are not. Neither are we worthy of Christ's wondrous love for us. But Christ loves us— not according to our worthiness—but according to the riches of His own loving heart! So should it be with our giving of friendship—not as the person deserves— but after the measure of our own character.

These are illustrations enough to show what it may *cost* to be a friend. When we receive another into this *sacred relationship*, we do not know what *responsibility* we are taking upon ourselves, what *burdens* it may be ours to carry in being faithful, what *sorrows* our love may cost us. It is a sacred thing, therefore, to take a new friend into our lives. We accept a solemn responsibility when we do so. We do not know what *burdens* we may be assuming, what *sacrifices* we may unconsciously be pledging ourselves to make, what *sorrows* may come to us through the one to whom we are opening our heart. We should choose our friends, therefore, thoughtfully, wisely, prayerfully—but when we have pledged our love, we should be faithful, *whatever* the cost may be!

The Sin of Being a Discourager

"So I made up my mind that I would not make another painful visit to you." 2 Corinthians 2:1

There are some people who always look at the *dark side*. They find all the *shadows* in life, and persist in walking in them. They make darkness for others wherever they may go—never brightness. These people do a great deal of harm in the world. They make all of life *harder* for those they influence. They make *sorrow* harder to bear, because they exaggerate it, and because they blot out all the *stars* of *hope* and *comfort* which God has set to shine in this *world's night*. They make *burdens* appear heavier because, by their discouraging philosophy, they leave the heart beneath the burden less strong and brave to endure. They make *life's battles* harder because by their ominous forebodings, they paralyze the arm that wields the sword. The whole effect of the life of these people—is to *discourage* others; to find *unpleasant* things and point them out; to discover *dangers* and tell about them; to look for *difficulties* and *obstacles* and proclaim them.

A thoughtful man was asked to contribute to the erection of a monument to one of these discouragers, and replied: "Not a penny. I am ready to contribute toward building monuments to those who make us *hope*—but I will not give a penny to those who live to make us *despair*." He was right. Men who make life harder for us, cannot be called benefactors. The true benefactors are those who show us *light* in our darkness, *comfort* in our sorrows, *hope* in our despair.

We all need to be *strengthened* and *inspired* for life's difficult experiences; never weakened and disheartened. If we meet others cast down and discouraged, it is our duty as their friends not to make their trials and cares seem as *large* as we can—but rather to point out to them the *silver lining* in their clouds, and to put new *hope* and *courage* in their hearts. If we find others in *sorrow*, it is our duty not to tell them merely how sorry we are for them, how we pity them—but coming close to them in love, to whisper in their ears the strong *comforts of divine grace*, to make them stronger to endure their sorrow. If we find others in the midst of difficulties and conflicts, faint and ready almost to yield—it is our duty not merely to bemoan with them the severity and hardness of their battles, and then to leave them to go on to sure defeat—but to *inspire* them to bravery and victory!

It is of vital importance that we learn this lesson—if we want to be true helpers of others in their lives. If we have only *sadness* to give to men and women—we have no right to go among them. It is only when we have something that will bless them and lift up their hearts and give them glimpses of bright and beautiful things to live for—that we are truly commissioned to go forth as evangels into the world.

It is better that we should not sing of *sadness*—if our song ends there. There are enough *sad notes* already floating in the world's air, moaning in men's ears. We should sing only and always of hope, joy, and cheer. Jeremiah had a right to weep, for he sat amid the crumbling ruins of his country's prosperity, looking upon the swift and resistless approach of woes which might have been averted. Jesus had a right to weep on the Mount of Olives, for His eye saw the terrible doom coming upon the people He loved, after doing all in His power to avert the doom which sin and unbelief were dragging down upon them.

But not many of us are called to live amid grief like that which broke the heart of Jeremiah. And as of Jesus, we know what a Preacher of *hope* He was wherever He went. Our mission must be to carry to men, not tidings of grief and doom—but joy and good news. People are saying to us: "Give us your hopes, your joys, your sunshine, your life, your uplifting truths; we have sorrows, tears, clouds, ills, chains, doubts enough of our own!"

This is the mission of Christianity in the world—to help men to be *victorious*, to whisper *hope* wherever there is despair, to give *cheer* wherever there is discouragement. It goes forth to *open*prisons, to *loosen* chains, and to *free* captives. Its symbol is not only a cross—that is one of its symbols, telling of the price of our redemption, telling of love that died—but its final symbol is an*open grave*, open and empty! We know what that means. It tells of life, not of death; of life victorious over death. We must not suppose that its promise is only for the final resurrection; it is for resurrection every day, every hour, over all death. It means unconquerable, unquenchable, indestructible, immortal *life*—at every point where *death* seems to have won a victory. Defeat anywhere is simply impossible, if we are in Christ and if

Christ is in us. It is just as true of the Christ in us—as it was of the Christ who went down into Joseph's tomb, that He cannot be held captive by death.

It follows that there never can be a *loss* in a Christian's life, out of which a *gain* may not come, as a plant from a buried seed. There can never be a *sorrow* out of which a *blessing* may not be born. There can never be a *discouragement* which may not be made to yield some fruit of *strength*.

If, therefore, we are true and loyal messengers of Christ, we can never be *prophets of gloom*, disheartenment, and despair. We must ever be heralds of hope. We must always have good news to tell. There is a gospel which we have a right to proclaim to everyone, whatever his sorrow may be. In Christ there is always hope, a secret of *victory*, a power to transmute loss into *gain*, to change defeat to *victory*, to bring *life* from death. We are living worthily—only when we are living victoriously ourselves at every point, when we are inspiring and helping others to live victoriously, and when our lives are songs of *hope* and *gladness*, even though we sing out of tears and pain!

Summer Gathering for Winter's Needs

"He who *gathers crops in summer* is a wise son, but he who sleeps during harvest is a disgraceful son." Proverbs 10:5. So the inspired proverb tells us. In its simplest form the reference is to the gathering and laying up of food in the summer days. There is a season when the harvest is waving in the fields, when the fruits hang heavy on trees and vines, when earth's good things wait to be gathered. That is the time when men must be diligent—if they would lay in store for their *winter's needs*. Not long does the *opportunity* wait. No sooner are the fruits ripe—than they begin to decay and fall off. No sooner is the harvest golden—than it begins to perish. *Winter* follows *summer*. Then there are no *fruits* on the trees or vines, no *harvests* waving on the fields. The hungry man cannot go out *then* to gather food, and if he has not gathered in *summer*—he must suffer hunger.

But the *principle* has wide application. Life has its *summers* and its *winters*—its times of health, plenty, opportunity; then its times of sickness or need; and these seasons of need must survive, from the stores laid up in the days of abundance. *Youth* is a summer. It is a time for the forming of *habits*, for the knitting of the muscles and sinews of *character*, for the making of *friendships*. Later on comes "real life," with its duties, its responsibilities, its struggles, its sorrows, its losses. But he who has gathered in life's *summer*—shall not lack in life's *winter*. A youth-time diligently spent in improvement, prepares one for whatever comes in the sterner years; while every opportunity *wasted* in youth—-is a risk for misfortune, or failure in later life.

The same law applies in *spiritual* life. In our time of quietness and security, we may *store up* in our hearts, the resources we shall need to draw upon for meeting temptation. Childhood and early youth in a true Christian home, are sheltered in a large measure from stern assaults and bitter conflicts. The *atmosphere* is kindly and congenial. The *influences* are helpful. There is a *mother's shoulder* to cry on—and a *father's hand* to lead and protect. The *family altar* holds all the household close to God's feet. The sin of the world outside, washes against the very threshold, the spray of its tide dashing against the windows; yet within the sacred walls—there is a holy life, unperturbed, unstained, loving, gentle, and sincere. The child that grows up amid these holy influences, is sheltered from the temptations that make the world outside such a perilous a place in which to live. This is *life's summer.*

But the *winter* eventually comes. No young person can live always in such a shelter. The time comes, sooner or later—when the children must go out to face the temptations of the world. It is possible, however, in the days of quiet in the home—to so gather spiritual resources in the heart—that in the conflicts of later days, the life shall be safe.

When men build a great ship to go upon the sea, they pile away in its keel, tremendous strength, staunch ribs, immense beams and stays, and heavy steel plates. They at building the vessel for the ocean, and they make it strong enough to endure the wildest tempests.

In like manner, human lives should be built in the home in the days of youth—not merely for the sweet experiences of the home itself—but to meet the sternest buffetings and the severest testings that any possible future may bring. *Principles* should he fixed in the heart so firmly—that nothing can ever swerve the life from them. *Habits* should be so wrought into the conduct—that nothing can change them. *Conscience* should be so trained—that it shall do its duty in the greatest stress, without wavering.

The *lesson* is for the *young.* In the bright sunny days—they should gather into their lives, stores of moral and spiritual strength from which to draw—when they go forth to encounter the world's fierce temptations. *Memory* should be filled with the Words of God. The great essential principles of Christianity should be so fixed in their minds—that no assaults of skepticism can make them doubt. The fundamental laws of *morality* should be settled in their very soul—as the laws of their own life. Their *spiritual habits* should be so firmly fixed—that they will carry their faith with them out into the world—as they carry their faces or their throbbing hearts. Into the ship of their lives, their characters, they should stockpile massive strength, which nothing can possibly overcome.

The same is true of preparation for *sorrow.* We are not to forecast trouble—and yet we are to live so that when trouble comes, we shall be prepared for it. The *wise virgins* were not left in darkness as were their foolish sisters, when their own lamps went out because they had no *reserve* of oil in their vessels. If we have a store of divine promises and comforts hidden in our hearts, gathered and laid away there during the bright days—we shall never be left in *darkness* however suddenly the *shadow* may fall upon us. Here we see the benefit of memorizing Scripture in childhood. People often ask, "What is the use of teaching children Scripture texts which they cannot understand?" The use will appear, by and by.

In a new building, the workmen were observed putting gas-pipes and electric wires into the walls. There seemed to be no use in this. It would be months before there could be any need of light or heat. Yes—but the time to put them in is now, when the house is in the process of construction. They will be covered up and hidden behind the plastering and the woodwork. But when the house is occupied, it will be necessary only to push a button—and the electric lights will fill the rooms with light; or to turn a knob—and the flame would be there for heat or cooking.

There may seem to be no use in putting into a child's memory, words it cannot understand. They make no impression at present. They give out no light. But they are fixed in the life, and someday there will come sorrow. It *will* grow dark. Then from these words will flash out the sweet light of divine love, pouring the soft radiance of heavenly comfort—upon the night of grief.

A touching story is told of a young man who was rapidly and surely losing his eyesight. The physicians told him that he would be able to see but for a few months. At once, accompanied by a sister, he set out to travel over Europe, taking a *last look* at the beautiful things of this world, before his eyes would be closed forever. He wished to have his memory stored with *lovely pictures* of mountains, lakes, and waterfalls, of fine buildings and works of art, so that when he would no longer be able to see—he might have these beautiful visions in his soul, to lighten his gloom.

We should walk in the light—while we have the light. We should train ourselves to see all the beauty we can find in God's works and Word. We should gather into our souls—all the love, joy, and gladness that we can store there, *while we may*. Then when the *night* settles about us—we shall have *light* within.

In Rose Porter's little book, 'Summer Driftwood for the Winter Fire,' the grandfather's counsel to the child is "Annie, the *flowers* will fade, the *sunshine* will be hidden when the winter storm-clouds come, and the song *birds* will fly away. Find something *lasting*. Begin to gather wood now—that will warm the heart when the winter of life comes."

No wiser counsel could be given to the young. Let the sunshine into your hearts in the bright days—God's sunshine of love and truth. Read good, wholesome, helpful books that will leave great and honorable thoughts in your memory. Especially read the Bible, and store its words in your mind. Do beautiful things, things of love, of unselfishness, of helpfulness, things that are true, honorable, just, pure, and lovely. Nothing darkens life's winter days—as do *memories of sinful things*. Nothing makes life so sweet in old age—as does the memory of right and good things done through the years.

Gather about you, too, in the sunny days—gentle and worthy *friends*. Be sure they are worthy, for unworthy friends often make bitterness and sorrow for the dark days of those whom they disappoint. Above all, gather into your soul—the sweet friendship of Jesus Christ, and let His words bless your life and fill and enrich your heart! Then, when the *winter days* come, the memories of all these precious things will abide, and will shine like soft lamps in the gloom. Such *gathering* in the *summer* days of life—will make the *winter* cheerful and bright within, even with storm and darkness outside!

Christs *Reserve* in Teaching

"Who is it he is trying to teach? To whom is he explaining his message? To children weaned from their milk, to those just taken from the breast? For precept must be upon precept, precept upon precept; line upon line, line upon line; here a little, and there a little " Isaiah 28:9-10

"I have much more to say to you—more than you can now bear." John 16:12

Christ never teaches us more rapidly—than we can receive His lessons. It was in the midst of His most confidential talk with His disciples, that He said He had much more to say to them, more than they could now bear. All wise teaching must be from the simplest rudiments, up to the more complex knowledge. The mind is not capable of comprehending the higher elements until it has been developed and trained. Then *truth* itself is *progressive*, and the pupil is not prepared to receive the *advanced* lessons—until he has mastered the *rudiments*.

In like manner, *spiritual truths* can be received—only as we come to experiences for which they are adapted. There are many of the divine promises which we can never claim, and whose blessedness we cannot realize—until we come to the points in life for which they were specially given.

For example: "In the time of *trouble*—He shall hide me in His pavilion" (Psalm 27:5). This word can mean nothing to the child playing with his toys, or to the young man or woman walking in sunny paths, without a care or a trial. It can be understood only by one who is in trouble.

Or, take this word: "My grace is sufficient for you" (2 Corinthians 12:9). It was given as an answer to a prayer for the removal of an unrelenting trial. It meant divine strength to offset human weakness, and it cannot be received until there is a sense of need.

Christ stands beside a happy young Christian and says: "I have a precious word to give you, one that shines with the beauty of divine love—but you cannot bear it yet." The disciple moves on along life's sunny path, and by and by comes into the shadows of sorrow or trouble. Again Jesus stands beside him and says: "*Now* I can give you the word I withheld before: "My grace is sufficient for you!" *Then* the promise glows with light and love.

There is a very large part of the Bible which can be received by us only when we come into the places for which the words were given. There are promises for *weakness*—which we can never get while we are strong. There are words for times of *danger*—which we can never know while we need no protection, There are consolations for *sickness*—whose comfort we can never get, while we are in robust health. There are promises for times of *loneliness* when men walk in solitary ways—which never can come with real meaning to us, while loving companions are by our side. There are words for *old age*—which we never can appropriate for ourselves along the years of youth, when the arm is strong, the blood warm, and the heart brave.

God cannot show us the *stars*—while the *sun* shines in the heavens; and He cannot make known to us the precious things of love that He has prepared for our *nights*—while it is yet *day* about us. Christ says to us then, "I have much more to say to you—more than you can now bear." We could not understand them now. But by and by, when we come into places of need, of sorrow, of weakness, of human failure, of loneliness, of sickness, of old age—*then* He will tell us these *other things*—and they will be full of joy for our hearts. When *night* comes, He will show us the*stars!*

Older Christians understand this. There are many things in the Bible which had little meaning for them in life's earlier days—but which one by one have shone bright and beautiful along the years—as stars come out in the evening sky when the sun fades from the heavens. Even in childhood, the *words* were said over and over—but they were repeated thoughtlessly, because there had been no *experience* to prepare the heart to receive them. Then one day there crept a *dark shadow* over the life, and in the shadow—the long familiar words began for the first time, to have a meaning. Other experiences of care, trial, and loss followed—and the precious words became more and more real. Now, in old age, as the sacred texts are repeated, they are the very rod and staff to the trembling, trusting spirit.

Thus as life goes on, the *meaning* of Christ's words comes out clearer and clearer, until the child's heedless repetition of them—becomes the utterance of the faithful and trust of the strong man's very soul.

We cannot bear now, the revealing of our own future. Christ knows it all. When a young Christian comes to His feet and says, "I will follow You, wherever You lead me" (Matt. 8:19), the Master knows what that promise means. But He does not reveal the knowledge to His happy disciple. People sometimes say they wish they could look on into the future years and see all that will come to them. But would this be a blessing? Would it make them happier? Could they shape their course better—if they knew all that shall befall them—the struggles, the victories, the defeats, the joys and sorrows, the failures of bright hopes, just how long they will live?

Surely it is better we should *not* know our future. So the word of the Master is continually: "I have much more to say to you—more than you can now bear." Only as we go on, step by step—does He disclose to us His will and plan for our lives. Thus the *joys* of life do not dazzle us—for our hearts have been chastened to receive them. The *sorrows* do not overwhelm us—because each one brings its own special comfort with it. But if we had known in advance of the *coming joys* and prosperities, the exultation might have made us heedless of duty and overly self-confident, thus missing the blessing that comes only to simple, trusting faith. If we had known of the *struggles* and *trials* before us, we might have been disheartened, thus failing in courage to endure. In either case, we could not have borne the revelation, and it was in tenderness and kindness to us—that the Master withheld it.

We could not bear the many things Christ has to tell us about *heaven*—and therefore He does not tell them to us. The blessedness, if disclosed now—would dazzle and blind our eyes! The light must be let in upon us, little by little, so as not to harm us. Then if heaven were within our sight, as we toil and struggle and suffer here—the bliss would so excite us, that we would be unfit for duty!

A traveler tells of returning to France after a long voyage to India. As soon as the sailors saw the *shores* of their own land, they became incapable of attending to their duties on the ship. When they came into port and saw their friends on the dock, the excitement was so intense that another crew had to take their place. Would it not be so with us—if heaven were visible from earth?*Its blessedness* would win us away from our duties! The sight of its splendors would so charm and entrance us—that we would weary of earth's painful life. If we could see our loved ones on heaven's shore, we would not be content to stay here to finish our work! Surely it is better that *more* has not been revealed. The *veiled* glory does not dazzle us, and yet faith realizes it, and is sustained by the precious hope in its struggles through the *night of earthly life*—until at last, the morning breaks.

This is the great *law of divine revealing*. We learn Christ's teaching—as fast as we are able to bear it. So we may wait in patient faith when *mysteries* confront us, or when *dark shadows* lie on our path, confident that He who knows all, has in gentle love, withheld from us for the time, the revelation we crave—because we could not yet endure the knowledge!

In Time of Loneliness

"*Surely I am with you always*--to the very end of the age." Matthew 28:20

Loneliness is one of the most pathetic of human experiences. The *yearning for companionship* is one of the deepest of all yearnings. The religion of Christ has something to meet every human need; what is its blessing for loneliness? We may turn to the Master's own life for an answer to our question. He met all the experiences that ever become ours, and He found for Himself the best there is to be found in the *divine love*—to meet His experiences. Thus He showed us what we may find in our times of need, and how we may find it.

Christ's loneliness was one of the most bitter elements of His earthly sorrow. His very *greatness of character,* made it impossible for Him to have any real companionship in this world. Besides, those whom He came to bless and save, rejected Him. The only human relief to His loneliness along the years of His public ministry—was in the love of His chosen friends—and this was most unsatisfactory.

But we know where He ever turned for solace and comfort in His experiences. After a day of pain and suffering, He would climb the mountain and spend the night in communion with His Father, returning in the morning renewed and strong for another day of sweet life and service. In His darkest hour, He said that though left alone as to human companionship, He was not alone because *His Father was with Him.*

The comfort of our Lord's heart in His loneliness, is for us, too—if we are walking in His steps. We, too, have our experiences of loneliness in this world, and we, too, may have the blessed companionship that shall fill the emptiness. In a certain sense—all of life is lonely. Even with sympathetic companions all about us, there is an *inner life* which each one of us lives *altogether alone.* We must make our own *choices* and decisions. We must meet our own *questions* and answer them ourselves. We must fight our own *battles*, endure our own *sorrows*, carry our own*burdens.* Friendship may be very close and tender—but there is a sanctuary of each life—into which even the holiest friendship may not enter. Blessed are they who in this *aloneness* can say, "Yet I am not alone, because the Father is with me!"

God's is the *only* friendship that can really meet all our soul's deep needs and cravings. *Human* companionship helps us at a few points; but the divine friendship has its blessing for every experience. We never shall be left alone, when we have Christ. When other helpers fail and comforts flee—He will ever stand close beside us. When other faces fade out of view—His will shine out with gentle love, pouring its light upon us.

There are special experiences of loneliness in every life—for which Christ is needed. YOUTH is one of these times. Youth seems happy and lighthearted. Companions swarm all around it. But often a young person feels lonely even amid such scenes and friendships. All of life is new to him. As his soul awakens, a thousand questions arise demanding answers. He is in a world with a*thousand paths*—and he must choose in which one he will walk. Everything is mysterious. There are *perils* lurking on all sides. *Choices* must be made. *Lessons* must be learned. All is new, and at every step the voice is heard, "You have not passed this way before" (Joshua 3:4). This loneliness of inexperience, when a young soul is taking its earliest steps in life—is one of the most trying and painful feelings of all the years. If Christ is not his companion, then, lonely and perilous indeed, is the way! But if He walks beside the young soul in its inexperience, all is well.

There are those who are lonely, because they are homeless. It is impossible to estimate too highly—the value and the helpfulness of a true home of love. Home is a *shelter.* Young lives *nest*there—and find warmth and protection. There is also *guidance* in a true Christian home. Many of life's hardest questions are answered by a wise mother or father. Blessed is that young man or young woman who takes every perplexity, every mystery, every doubt or fear and every hunger—home to the sacredness of love's sanctuary, and gets there sympathy, patient counsel, and true guidance.

Home has also its blessed companionship. It is the only place where we are absolutely sure of each other—and do not need to be on our *guard*. Youth has its unspeakable *longings*, its deep*hungers*, its cravings for *tenderness*. In the true home, these are all met. Those who have such a home—do not realize the half of its value to them. It is the very *shadow of Christ's wings* over their lives, the very cleft of the Rock, the very *bosom of divine love!* Life's loneliness means far less to them— while home shields them and blesses them with its companionship and its patient, wise, helpful, nourishing love.

But sometimes the home is pulled down over youth—and its *shelter* broken up. Few things are sadder than *homelessness*. Loneliness begins to be really felt—when the home is gone, when there is no longer a wise and loving *mother* to give her counsel in your inexperience, to lay her hand on your head in blessing; to listen to your questions and answer them; to restrain your impetuous spirit; to quiet you when you are perturbed and when your peace is broken; to lead you through perplexing paths; to fill your hungry heart with the comfort of love when you long for sympathy and companionship. Bitter indeed is the sense of loneliness—when a young person, used to all that a mother's love means—turns away from a *mother's grave* to miss thereafter the blessings that have been so much in the past. Nothing earthly will in any full measure, compensate for the loss. Other human friendships may be very precious—but they will not give back*home* with its shelter, its affection, its trust, its guidance, its soothing, its security.

But blessed is that life which in earthly homelessness can say, "Yet I am not alone, because *Christ* is with me!" Blessed is that loneliness of homelessness which has *Christ* to fill the emptiness. With Christ unseen—yet loved and made real to the heart by love and faith—even a room in a boarding house may become a home, a sanctuary of peace, *a shelter of divine love!*

Another time of special loneliness, is when *sorrow* strips off the friendships of life. *Old age* is an illustration. Old people are often very lonely. Once they were the center of groups of friends and companions who clustered about them. But the *years* brought their changes. Now the old man stands alone. Still the streets are full—but where are the faces of forty or fifty years ago? There is a memory of vacant chairs, of marriage altars with the unbindings and separation that follow. The old faces are gone. It is the young life that now fills the home, the streets, the church—and the old people are lonely because their old friends are gone.

Yet the *aged Christian* can surely say, "I am not alone!" No changes in life can take Jesus away. He is the Companion of life's feebleness. He loves His aged people. There is a special promise for them: "Even to your *old age* and gray hairs I am he, I am he who will *sustain* you. I have *made* you and I will *carry* you; I will *sustain* you and I will *rescue* you!" (Isaiah 46:4). For the Christian, old age is very near to *glory*. It will not be long until the aged Christian reaches *home*—to stand again amid the circle of beloved holy ones who blessed their youth and early years.

But not only *old* people are left lonely by life's changes. Sorrow touches *all ages*, and if we have not Christ, when other friends are taken, we shall be desolate indeed. Blessed is that life which, when human friends are taken away, finds the friendship of Christ all-filling, all-satisfying, and can say, "Yet I am not alone—for Christ is with me!"

The loneliest of all human experiences is that of *dying*. We cannot die in groups, not even two by two; we must die alone. Human hands must unclasp ours as we enter the valley of shadows. Human faces must fade from our vision—as we pass into the mists. "I cannot see you!" said one who was dying, as the loved ones stood about his bed. So will it be with each one of us in our turn. *Human* love cannot go beyond the edge of the valley. But we need not be alone—even in that deepest of all loneliness; for if we are Christ's, we can say, "Yet I am not alone, because my Savior is with me!"

When the *human* hands unclasp, His *divine* hands will clasp ours the more firmly. When beloved human faces fade out, His lovely countenance will shine above us in all its glorious brightness. When we must creep out of the bosom of human affection, it will be only into the clasp of the everlasting arms, into the bosom of Christ! Death's loneliness, will thus be filled with divine companionship.

The inference from all this, is our *absolute need* of the friendship and companionship of Christ, without which we can only sink away in life's loneliness and eternally perish! One reason, no doubt, why our lives are so full of experiences of need—is that we may learn to walk with Christ. If earth's human companionships satisfied us, and if we never lost them—we might not care for Christ's friendship. If earth's homes were perfect, and if they never crumbled—we might not grow homesick for *heaven!*

In the Everlasting Arms

"The eternal God is your refuge, and underneath are *the everlasting arms!"* Deuteronomy 33:27

There are *two sides* to a Christian life.

One is the *active* side. We are urged to faithfulness in all duty, to activity in all service, to victory in all struggle, to work out our own salvation with fear and trembling.

But there is another side. We are to trust, to have quietness and confidence, to repose on God. It is well that we sometimes think of the latter aspect of our Christian faith. This is well presented to us in a Bible verse which says, "Underneath are the everlasting arms."

The picture suggested is that of a little child, lying in the strong arms of a father who is able to withstand all storms and dangers. We think of John lying upon

Christ's bosom. At the two extremes of life, *childhood* and *old age*—the promise comes with special assurance. "He shall gather the *lambs* in His arms, and carry them in His bosom" (Isaiah 40:11), is a word for the children. "Even to your *old age* and gray hairs I am he, I am he who will *sustain* you. I have *made* you and I will *carry* you; I will *sustain* you and I will *rescue* you!" (Isaiah 46:4), brings its blessed comfort to the aged. God comes to us first in our infancy, through our mothers, who carried us in their arms. Yet they are only dim revelations of God for a time. They leave us after teaching us a little of God's tenderness—but God Himself remains when they are gone, and His arms never unclasp!

The thought of *God's embracing arms* is very suggestive. What does an *arm* represent? What is the thought suggested by the *arm of God enfolded around His child?* The language is human. The Scriptures speak continually of God in this way. They tell us of His *eyes* looking down to behold His people—that He never slumbers nor sleeps; meaning that His watchful care never intermits. They tell us that He *listens* to earth's cries, and *hears* the sighing of the oppressed, and the groaning of the prisoner in his dungeon; meaning that He hears our cries of distress. They speak of His *wiping away tears*, as a mother would dry a child's tears; meaning that He comforts His people in their sorrow. They represent Him as *holding us by the right hand*, as a father holds his child's hand in his own, when it walks over dangerous places; meaning that His guidance is personal and strong.

All these, and like statements in *human language* of what God does for His people—are efforts to explain to us by means of human acts with which we are familiar, His wonderful care and kindness. Thus the figure of the *arm* as applied to God—is to be interpreted by what it would mean in human friendship.

One meaning is **protection**. A father puts his arm about his child when it is in *danger*. God protects His children, "With your *mighty arm* You redeemed Your people" (Psalm 77:15). "Be our *strength* every morning, and our salvation in time of trouble" (Isaiah 33:2). "His arm brought salvation" (Isaiah 59:16).

Life is full of *peril*. There are *temptations* on every hand! *Enemies* lurk in every shadow—enemies strong and swift! Many people think of *death* with fear, dreading to meet it. But *life* has far more perils—than death! It is easy and safe to die—when one has lived a holy life. But it is hard to live. Yet we are assured that "life" cannot separate us from the love of God. "Underneath are the everlasting arms!"

Another meaning is **affection**. The father's arm drawn around a child—is a token of *love*. The child is held in the father's bosom, near his heart. The shepherd carries the *lambs* in his bosom. John lay on Jesus' bosom. The mother holds the child in her bosom, because she loves it. This picture of God embracing His children in His arms—tells of His love for them. His love is tender, close, intimate. He holds them in the place of *affection*.

It is especially in the time of danger or suffering—that the mother thus embraces her child. She takes him up when he has fallen and has hurt himself—and comforts him by holding him in her arms, and pressing him to her bosom. "As one whom his mother comforts—so will I comfort you" (Isaiah 66:13), is a divine word. A mother said that her little sick one, had scarcely been out of her arms for three days and nights. Holding in the arms—is a peculiar privilege of love—for times of pain and suffering. It tells therefore of our heavenly Father's tenderness towards His own when they are in distress.

Another thought suggested by an arm is **strength**. The arm is a symbol of strength. A mother's arm may be frail physically—but love makes it strong. When it is folded about a feeble child, all the power of the universe cannot tear the child away. We know what it is in human friendship, to have one upon whose arm we can lean with confidence. There are some people whose mere presence seems to give us a sense of security. We believe in them. In their quiet peace, there is a strength which imparts itself to all who lean upon them. Every true human friend, is more or less a strength to us. Yet the surest, strongest human strength—is but a fragment of the divine strength. His arm is omnipotence. "In the Lord Jehovah is *everlasting strength*" (Isaiah 26:4). His is an arm that can never be broken. Out of this clasp—we never can be taken. "I give them eternal life, and they will never perish—ever! No one will snatch them out of My hand!" John 10:28

Another suggestion is **endurance**. The arms of God are "everlasting." Human arms grow weary even in love's embrace; they cannot forever press the child to the bosom. Soon they lie folded in death. A husband stood by the coffin of his beloved wife after only one short year of wedded happiness. The clasp of that love was very sweet—but how brief a time it lasted, and how desolate was the life that had lost the precious companionship! A little baby two weeks old, was left motherless. The mother clasped the child to her bosom and drew her feeble arms about it in one loving embrace; the little one never more will have a mother's arm around it. So *pathetic* is human life with its broken affections, its little moments of love, its embraces that are torn away in one hour. But these are everlasting arms—these arms of God. They shall never unclasp!

There is another important suggestion in the word "underneath." Not only do the arms of God *embrace* His child—but they are *underneath* — *always* underneath. That means that *we* can never sink—for these arms will ever be beneath us, wherever we may be found. Sometimes we say the *waters of trouble* are very deep; like great floods they roll over us. But still and forever, underneath the deepest floods—are these everlasting arms. We cannot sink below them—or out of their clasp!

And when *death* comes, and every earthly thing is gone from beneath us, and we sink away into what seems darkness—out of all human love, out of warmth and gladness and life—into the gloom and strange mystery of death—still it will only be—into the everlasting arms!

When *Jesus* was dying, He said, "Father, into Your hands I commit My spirit" (Luke 23:46). He found the everlasting arms underneath Him when His spirit left the torn body. *Stephen* died, praying, "Lord Jesus, receive my spirit" (Acts 7:59). To a believer, dying is simply breathing the life—into the embrace of God. We shall find the divine arms underneath us. Death cannot separate us from the love of God.

This view of the divine care is full of inspiration and comfort. We are not saving ourselves. A strong One, the mighty God—holds us in His omnipotent clasp! We are not tossed like a leaf on life's wild sea—driven at the mercy of wind and wave. We are in divine keeping. Our security does not depend upon our own feeble, wavering faith—but upon the omnipotence, the love, and the faithfulness of the unchanging, the eternal God! We can never sink away in any flood. No power in the universe can snatch us out of His hands. Neither death nor life, nor things present, nor things to come, can separate us from His love!

I Am the Only One Left!

Elijah replied, "I have been very zealous for the Lord God Almighty. The Israelites have rejected your covenant, broken down your altars, and put your prophets to death with the sword. *I am the only one left*, and now they are trying to kill me too!" 1 Kings 19:10

Elijah at a certain great crisis, thought he was the only one left to stand for God. There were others—but he did not know of them. He was indeed the only one in the *field* for God. He stood alone, one man against and *evil king* and *false priests* and *sinful people*. It was a splendid heroism.

There come times in the lives of all who are Christians—when they must stand alone for God, without companionship, perhaps without sympathy or encouragement. Here is a young person, the only one of his family who has confessed Christ. He takes Him as His Savior and then stands up before the world and vows to be His and to follow Him. He goes back to his home. The members of his home circle are very dear to him—but none of them are Christians, and he must stand alone for Christ among them. Perhaps they *oppose* him—in his following Christ. In varying degrees, this many times is the actual experience. Perhaps they are only *indifferent*, making no opposition, only quietly watching his life to see if he is consistent. In any case, however, he must stand alone for Christ, without the help that comes from companionship.

Or it may be in the *workshop* or in the *school* that the young Christian must stand alone. He returns from the Lord's table to his weekday duties, full of noble impulses—but finds himself the only Christian. His companions are ready to sneer, and they point the *finger of scorn* at him, with irritating epithets. Or they even persecute him in petty ways. At the least—they are not Christ's friends, and he as a follower of the Master—finds no sympathy among them in his new life. He must stand alone in his discipleship, conscious all the while that *unfriendly eyes* are upon him. Many a young or older Christian, finds it very hard to be the only one to stand for Christ in the place of his daily work.

This aloneness puts upon one a great responsibility. Perhaps you are the only Christian in your *home*. You are the only witness Christ has in your house, the only one through whom He may reveal His love, His grace, His holiness. You are the only one to represent Christ in your family, to show to them the beauty of Christ, the sweetness and gentleness of Christ, to do there the works of Christ—the things He would do if He lived in your home. If you falter in your loyalty, if you fail in your duty, your loved ones may be lost, and the blame will be yours; their blood will be upon you.

In like manner, if you are the only Christian in the shop, the store, or the office where you work, a peculiar responsibility rests upon you, a responsibility which no other one shares with you. You are Christ's only witness in your place. If you do not testify there for Him, there is no other one who will do it.

Miss Havergal tells of her experience in a girl's school of Dusseldorf. She went there soon after she had become a Christian and had confessed Christ. Her heart was very warm with love for her Savior, and she was eager to speak for Him. To her amazement, however, she soon learned that among the hundred girls in the school— that she was the *only* Christian. Her first feeling was one of dismay—she could not confess Christ in that great company of worldly ungodly companions. Her gentle, sensitive heart—shrank from a duty so hard. Her second thought, however, was that she could not refrain from confessing Christ. "I am the only one He has here!" she said. And this thought became a great source of strength and inspiration to her. She realized that she had a *mission* in that school—that she was Christ's witness there, His only witness, and that she dare not fail.

This same sense of responsibility, rests upon every thoughtful Christian who is called to be Christ's only witness in a place—in a home, in a community, in a store, or school, or shop, or social circle. He is Christ's only servant there—and he dare not be unfaithful. He is the one light set to shine there for his Master, and if his light is hidden, then the darkness will be unrelieved. So there is special inspiration in this consciousness of *being the only one* Christ has in a certain place.

There is a sense in which this is true also of everyone of us—all the time. We are always the only one Christ has at the particular place at which we stand. There may be thousands of other lives about us. We may be only one of a great company, of a large congregation, of a populous community. Yet each one of us has a *life* that is *alone* in its responsibility, in its danger, in its mission and duty. There may be a hundred others close beside me—but not one of them can take *my* place, or do *my* duty, or fulfill *my* mission, or bear *my* responsibility. Though every one of the other hundred, does his work and does it perfectly, *my* work waits for me—and if I do not do it—it will never be done.

We can understand how that if *Elijah* had failed God that day when he was the only one God had to stand for Him, the consequences would have been disastrous; the cause of God would have suffered irreparably. But are we sure that the calamity to

Christ's kingdom would be any less—if one of *us* should fail God in our lowly place, on any common day?

Stories are told of a child finding a little leak in the dike that shuts off the sea from *Holland*, and stopping it with his hand until help could come—staying there all night, holding back the floods with his little hand. It was but a tiny, trickling stream that he held back; yet if he had not done it—it would soon have become a torrent, and before morning the sea would have swept over all the land, submerging fields, homes, and cities. Between the sea and all this devastation, there was but a boy's hand. Had the child failed, the floods would have rolled in with their remorseless ruin! We understand how important it was that the boy should be *faithful* to his duty, since he was the only one God had that night—to save Holland.

But how do you know that your life may not stand someday, and be all that stands, between a *great flood of moral decay*—and broad, fair fields of beauty? How do you know that your failure in your lowly place and duty may not let in a *sea of disaster* which shall sweep away human hopes and joys, possibly human souls? The humblest of us dare not fail—for our *one life* is all God has at the point where we stand.

This truth of *personal responsibility* is one of tremendous importance. We do not escape it by being in a crowd, one of a family, or one of a congregation. No one but ourselves can live our lives, do our work, meet our obligation, bear our burdens. No one but ourselves can stand for us at last before God—to render an account of our deeds. In the deepest, most real sense—*each one of us lives alone!*

There is another phase of this lesson; *we are responsible only for our own life and duty*. The prophet thought his work had failed, because the overthrow of Baalism seemed incomplete. But God comforted him, by telling him of three other men who would come, each in his time, and do each his part of the work in destroying Baalism. Elijah's work had not failed—but it was only a *fragment* of the whole work.

The best work any of us do in this world—is but a *fragment*. We all enter into each other's work, and others in turn shall enter into ours and finish or carry on toward completion, what we have begun. Our duty is simply *to do well our own little part*. If we do that, we need never worry about the part we *cannot* do. That belongs to some other worker, coming after us—not to us at all.

So while we are alone in our *responsibility*—we need have no concern for anything but our own duty, our own little fragment of the Lord's work. The things *we* cannot do—some other one is waiting and preparing now to do—after the work has passed from our hand. There is comfort in this for any who fail in their efforts, and must leave tasks unfinished—which they had hoped to complete. The *finishing* is another person's mission.

"Let us not become *weary in well doing*--for *at the proper time we will reap a harvest,* if we do not give up." Galatians 6:9

Sometimes we are inclined to be discouraged in our Christian *life* and *work*. We ask, "Is it worthwhile to be holy, to keep God's commandments? What profit is there in godliness? Is it worthwhile to deny ourselves—in order to do good to others, to serve them? What comes of it all?"

Many of us are apt to have moods in which these questions press upon us with painful stress. It is well that we look into the matter—that we may be assured that it is worthwhile to do good, that there is profit in it.

There is an inspired word which says, "Let us not become weary in *well doing,* for at the proper time we will reap a harvest if we do not give up." What is meant by "well doing"? It is doing right, obeying God's commands, fashioning our lives after the pattern revealed by Him in His word. It is not *easy* to do good. It costs us many a battle. A life of well doing, implies a continual crucifying of *SELF. Evil inclinations* must be restrained. *Sinful desires* must be curbed. The *will* must be yielded to God's will. The *whole life* must be brought into subjection to a law which is spiritual and heavenly.

"Does it pay?" is the question. There are many people who do not put their lives under this *law of God,* who go on in the ways of *self-indulgence.* They put no curb on their *evil inclinations.* They let no divine command interfere with the exercise of their own *sinful desires.* As we look at these people, it seems to us perhaps, that they are happier than we are. They appear to get more out of life, than we do. It seems to us that we are denying ourselves, sacrificing our comfort, and *cutting off our right hands*—for nothing! *Sin* seems to have the advantage. *Worldliness* appears to pay the best. *Virtue* seems *dreary* and *costly* and *lonesome.* It does not have the *good time* that *self-indulgence* has. And sometimes we do get *weary in well doing*—because there appears to be no profit in it.

"Well doing" means also the doing of good to others. We are taught that if we are Christians, we must *not live for ourselves.* Love is the essence of the new life, and love is doing, giving, sacrificing—for the sake of others. Instead of trying to get out of the world all we can for ourselves—we are to give the world all we can possibly give it of blessing and good.

It is easy to see that such a life is *not natural,* and that is not in harmony with *human* feelings and tastes. Naturally we care for *ourselves* and for our own benefit and comfort. We do not incline to put ourselves out, to sacrifice our own convenience, to serve others. We might do it for one we love deeply—but the gospel requires us to love and serve, with all our capacity for serving—those who are not among our congenial friends—and even our enemies! An enemy who needs us—we must serve. Even the most debased human life that we find in our path—we must touch with our healing love, and help with the hands that have been given to Christ. We are required to hold our lives and all that we have—at the call of love and of human need. We

are to *bear one another's burdens*. We are to have *sympathy* with all sorrow and need, to be ever *touched* with a sense of the world's forlorn condition. This *law of Christian love* puts us down among men—just as Christ Himself was among men. He kept nothing back—for Himself. He never thought a thought nor breathed a breath—for Himself. He poured out the blessing of His holy life without limit—on everyone who came near Him, at last giving His very life-blood for the saving of sinful man.

That is what "well doing" means. And it is no wonder that some people stop and ask, "Is it worthwhile?" It is very natural for us to raise the question, whether the *giving* of all—is the best way to *gain* all; whether living altogether for others— is the way to make the most of our own lives, as we are required to do. We look at Christ, for example, and think of His rich, noble, blessed life. Never in any other human soul, were there such *treasures of manhood* stored, as in His. His was the sweetest, gentlest spirit—that ever looked out of human eyes! Never in any other mind—were there such intellectual powers; and never in any other *heart*—were there such depths and heights and breadths and lengths of love—as in His.

What did He do with His rich life? He turned away from the paths in which the world's great men had walked—and devoted Himself to the one work of *doing good to others*. He gave all He had to this work. He emptied Himself and made Himself poor—that others might be made rich. He exhausted His own strength—that the weak might be made strong. He poured out His own life-blood—that the dead might live.

Is that the best that *Christ* could have done with His wondrous life? His own friends thought not. They thought that He had *thrown away* His life.

Take those who are *following in Christ's footsteps*. A young American girl, having finished her college courses, came out with high honors. She had a keen mind, good social position, influential friends, a beautiful and happy home. Just then there came a call for missionary teachers to go to the South to work among the poor and needy. This young girl heard the call—and gave herself to this service. For two or three years she lived among the poor, teaching them, helping them, telling them too—of Christ. Then one day she contracted one of the *deadly diseases* rampant in the *ghettos* where she served her Lord—and soon she died among the impoverished, with no mother's hand to smooth her hair, or cool her fevered brow, or soothe her pain; with no mother's lips to kiss her before her earth's last farewell.

They brought her body back and buried it among her friends—but on almost every tongue was the sad complaint, "She had *wasted* her beautiful life. It ought to have been kept and used for service in more gentle, refined ways. It was *too rich a life* to be poured out in such costly ministry!" So they talked beside her coffin. But was that sweet life *wasted?* Could she have done anything better with it?

To all these questions, there comes as an answer—the promise that "*at the proper time we will reap a harvest* if we do not give up." It is not in vain that we continue our *well doing,* that we obey God's commandments, that we devote our lives in self-sacrificing service to others, for Christ's sake. What *seems* to be loss—is gain. The godly man may *seem* to have more trouble than his ungodly neighbor. His business may not *appear* to prosper as well. His ventures may fail. His faithfulness may bring him *enmity* from others, and even *persecution.*

But *life's accounts* are not always settled at once. *Harvest* does not immediately follow *sowing.* It is so in nature. There are days and months when the *seed seems* to have perished. Afterward, however, it yields *fruit.* It is the same in spiritual life. For a time, there may seem to be no *blessing* in well doing. But in the end, righteousness succeeds. "The one who sows to please the Spirit—from the Spirit will reap eternal life!" Galatians 6:8

Every *kindness* we do to another in the name of Christ—is the sowing of a good seed unto the Spirit. Every deed of *love,* every act of *unselfishness,* every *self-denial;* all the things we do to *help,* to *comfort,* or to *bless* others—are seeds which we sow to please the Spirit. "At the *proper time* we will reap a harvest!" For the present, it may not appear that any good or blessing comes from the *act* of love—or the *word* of kindness spoken. But the *seed* does not perish; it has in it an immortal germ.

The world about us is full of needs. One said the other day—that everything he was interested in, every piece of Christian work, every institution, was needing money. We all find it so. On every hand are calls for help. Either we must shut up our heart—or always be *giving* and *doing.* We dare not shut up our heart—that would mean moral and spiritual death. So we must always be *giving* and *doing.* We can keep nothing long, for ourselves. No sooner is it in our hands—than we are asked to give it out again—because *the Lord has need of it* in some other life, to meet some *need* of one of His little ones, or to do some *work of love* for Him. But we need never fear that anything—the *smallest thing* we do for another, with love for Christ in our heart—can fail of blessing.

Says one: "When men do anything for God—the very least thing—they never know where it will end, nor what amount of good it will do for Him. Love's secret, therefore, is to be *always doing things for God,* and not to mind because they are only little things."

Another says, "Oh, it is great, and there is no other greatness—to make some Christian work more fruitful, better, more worthy; to make some human heart a little wiser, stronger, happier, more blessed, less accursed."

We never know how *little benefactions of ours*—may bless a life and stay in it as a blessing forever! We know not, how even a small word may bless a life. We should always keep our *heart* and *hands* ready for whatever *little ministry* we may have an opportunity to render. The least word of *good cheer*—may start a song in a heart which shall sing on forever. The good may drop unconsciously from your lip and hand—and you may never think of it again, and yet it shall not be lost. It carries in it the life of God, and is immortal.

There is a *difference* in the way various people *give*—though the *gift* or *favor* or *act*—be precisely the same. One gives the *help* only; the other gives *part of himself* in the help. There are some very beautiful flowers that have no fragrance—but how much more a flower means—which has in it *perfume* as well as *loveliness!* We should give *ourselves* with our gifts. We should let part of our own lives—flow out with every deed of kindness we do.

Love is the *fragrance* of the flowers of the heart, and what we do in love—love for Christ and love for man—shall never be lost. The world will be richer and better for even the smallest deeds of Christlike love. We may not *reap the harvest* in this world—but beyond the skies, we shall gather the *sheaves* in our bosom! So then, though our lives are imperfect and evil, and our work is marred with sin—we know that the Master will accept the humblest thing we do for Him. He will cleanse our work and use it, even though it is only a *fragment*, in the building up of His kingdom!

Made in the USA
Middletown, DE
06 September 2022

73315249R00046